CHILDREN'S
ENCYCLOPEDIA
OF FLAGS

Claudia Martin

ARCTURUS

Picture Credits:
Every attempt has been made to clear copyright. Should there be any inadvertent omission,
please apply to the publisher for rectification.
Key: b–bottom, t–top, c–center, l–left, r–right

Académie de Grenoble: 121ctl; **Alamy:** 4cl (Action Plus Sports Images), 6-7 (funkyfood London, Paul Williams), 6cl (Heritage Image Partnership Ltd), 7bl (Classic Image), 8cr (Kay Roxby), 8-9 (Hemis), 10-11 (Prisma by Dukas Presseagentur GmbH), 14bl (Performance Image), 18br (Chuck Little), 34 (Universal Images Group North America LLC), 35tl (Han Yan/Xinhua), 42-43 (PA Images), 42cr (Joerg Boethling), 47tr (Melissa Jooste), 47cl (RIEGER Bertrand/hemis.fr), 55tl (Sueddeutsche Zeitung Photo), 58bc (Wenn Rights Ltd), 64bl (ton koene), 67cl (Mathias Rhode), 68cl (Kay Roxby), 74-75 (Hercules Milas), 74bl (Theo Moye), 82bl (Martin Lindsay), 86-87, 87br (ITAR-TASS News Agency), 98cl (agefotostock), 102tr (Petra Wegner), 110-111 (Reuters), 110bl (Nobuo Matsumura), 112bc (Eric Lafforgue), 122cl (Jon Arnold Images Ltd), 124bc (Eyal Bartov), 125tl (IanDagnall Computing); **Alex07:** 23cbr; **Amman City:** 63bl (Indolences); **Association MOTU HAKA/Association PATUTIKI:** 122bl (Sémhur); **BaronJaguar:** 23br; **B1mbo:** 125bl (Alakasam); **Bridgeman Images:** 8bl (Pictures from History), 70bl (© Lambeth Palace Library), 78tr (© Deutsches Historisches Museum), 90cl (© Gilder Lehrman Institute of American History), 106cl (Bridgeman), 123bc (Granger); **CARICOM:** 119bl; **Clindberg:** 12bl; **connormah:** 99tl (San José); **Dbenbenn:** 121brc; **Denelson83:** 19tl, 23tl, 121tc; **Dreamstime:** 124-125 (Darryn Schneider); **Froztbyte:** 47bl; **Fry1989:** 121tr; **Getty Images:** 14-15 (SRDJAN SUKI/AFP), 26-27 (Daniel Carde), 38br (Javier Soriano), 46-47 (Rodger Bosch), 66cl (DEA/J.E. SCHURR), 71cr (NurPhoto), 82-83 (Louisa Gouliamaki), 90-91 (Hill Street Studios), 102-103 (LatinContent), 118-119 (stockcam), 122-123 (Pedro Ugarte/AFP); **Gorivero:** 107tl (Government of Santa Cruz); **Great Brightstar:** 121tl, 121cbl; **Hogweard:** 71tl; **Huhsunqu:** 27cr; **iStock:** 28tr (jsanchex_bcn), 30bl (AlxeyPnferov), 32cr (mtcurado), 92cl (R Lolli Morrow), 100tr (nantonov), 106-107 (Global_Pics); **Jeltz:** 75br (Astrid Båhl/www.samediggi. no); **Johannes Rössel:** 23bc; **Kontrapunkt/The Nordic Council of Ministers and the Nordic Council:** 27tl; **Lexicon and GwenofGwened:** 23tc; **Mangwanani:** 24bl; **MapGrid:** 121bl; **Margaret Overbeck:** 90bl; **NASA/Neil A. Armstrong:** 21cr; **Nightstallion:** 121blc; **Nur-Sultan:** 67tl (HapHaxion); **Oneasy:** 6bl; **Pascal Lee:** 20bl (Minorax); **Pitlane02:** 15tl; **Rastrojo:** 23tr; **Shunsai Toshimasa:** 50tl; **Shutterstock:** 1 (ikiru), 4-5 (Leonard Zhukovsky), 5cr (Neil Bradfield), 10cl (viper-zero), 11tr (Dimitri Lamour), 12-13 (tong patong), 12tl (Neale Cousland), 13 (Denis Dubrovin), 14c (Marcin Kadziolka), 16-17 (Wiola Wiaderek), 16c (Michal Knitl), 17br (Marygrace_97), 18-19 (DreamSlamStudio), 18cl (inavanhataren), 20-21 (Leo Morgan), 20cl (AjayTvm), 22c (Millenius), 22bg (Shutting), 24-25 (Fedele Ferrara), 24cr (Leonid Altman), 25br (Alex Tihonovs), 26cl (The Art of Pics), 28, 32, 36, 40, 44, 48, 52, 56, 60, 64, 68, 72, 76, 80, 84, 88tc, 92tc, 96, 100c, 104, 108c, 112 (Peter Hermes Furian), 28bl (apdesign), 30cr (Thomas Wyness), 30-31 (PhiloPhotos), 32bl (ba55ey), 35br (GG Digital Arts), 36tr (Wang LiQiang), 36bl (Graeme Shannon), 38-39 (Juliya Shangarey), 38tl (Eduard Kyslynskyy), 40cr (Sergey Uryadnikov), 40bl (Atosan), 42tl (ravipat), 44cr (Neal Cooper), 44bl (zuhanna), 48tr (Sean Pavone), 48bl (Martinho Smart), 50-51 (daa.riaa), 50br (longtaildog), 52cr (kiwisoul), 52bl (icemanphotos), 54-55 (Nina Ross), 55br (Alexander A. Trofimov), 56cr (Leonid Andronov), 56bl (Knot Mirai), 58-59 (Evri Onefive), 58tl (Lena Serditova), 60c (RastoS), 60bl (Zaki Ghawas), 62-63 (arda savasciogullari), 62tr (Alberto Masnovo), 62bl (Wolfgang Cibura), 64c (Mikhail Gnatkovskiy), 66-67 (Alisher Primkulov), 68bc (Mark Breck), 70-71 (FenlioQ), 72cl (ImageBank4u), 72bc (Ondrej Prosicky), 76cl (Fernando Nicolas), 76cr (Boris Stroujko), 78-79 (Marcos del Mazo), 79c (Beach Creatives), 80cr (mfegus), 80bl (vvoe), 82tr (Yury Dmitrieriko), 84cl (eshma), 84bc (Calin Stan), 86tr (Wiktor Budniak), 88tr (f11photo), 88cl (Lee Prince), 88b (Maps Expert), 91br (Richard Laschon), 92tr (Alexey Seafarer), 92b (VectorShop), 94-95 (Alexander Sviridov), 94bl (Sophia Granchinho), 95c (Marc Bruxelle), 96tr (Richie Chan), 96bl (Fotos593), 98-99 (Martin Pelanek), 99bc (Andy Korteling), 100cl (James R. Schultz), 102bc (Christina Hemsley), 104cr (nvphoto), 104bl (Dudarev Mikhail), 108cr (Pete Niesen), 108bl (fritz16), 108bc (The Hornbills Studio), 110tr (Brian Donovan), 112tl (Tomacrosse), 114-115 (buteo), 114tl (Romaine W), 115bc (dominika zarzycka), 116 (brichuas), 116cl (Isabelle Kuehn), 116bc (Durk Talsma), 118tr (Vojtech Jirka), 119cr (Multiverse), 120 (tunasalmon), 120cr (P Rusky), 120cb (The Whiteview), 124cr (Reform-Furl581); **SKopp:** 121ctr; **Sodacan:** 95bl (Haida Nation), 103bl; **Statens Museum for Kunst:** 74tr (C.A. Lorentzen); **Tcfc2349:** 10bl, 121ctr, 121ctc; **Tobias Jakobs:** 117br (Abrax5), 121cbc; **Villacastrojimeno:** 23tbl; **Zscout370:** 23cbl (SeNeKa), 23cbc, 114bl (World Flag Database/Pacific Community), 121br. **All flags by Shutterstock except those listed above.**

All cover images are by Shutterstock. Front cover: main image ZENSE, tll Nostalgia for Infinity, tl Cavan-Images, c Calin Tatu, tr dogi, trr Gandi Purwandi; Back cover: Rawpixel.co.

ARCTURUS

This edition published in 2022 by Arcturus Publishing Limited
26/27 Bickels Yard, 151–153 Bermondsey Street,
London SE1 3HA

Copyright © Arcturus Holdings Limited

Author: Claudia Martin
Designer: Lorraine Inglis
Picture research: Paul Futcher
Consultant: Philip Steele
Editor: Becca Clunes
Design manager: Jessica Holliland
Editorial manager: Joe Haris

The flags shown here are those recognized by the United Nations. They are correct at the time of going to press.

ISBN: 978-1-3988-1109-6
CH0010089US
Supplier 42, Date 1221, Print run 11844

Printed in Singapore

CHILDREN'S ENCYCLOPEDIA OF FLAGS

CONTENTS

Introduction

Flags are flown from flagpoles, waved by excited sports fans, and planted on mountain peaks by exhausted climbers. Flags are usually a four-sided shape, with a bright and bold pattern. Most are made of cloth. Yet flags are always more than this: They are symbols and signals.

Symbols

A symbol is a pattern, picture, or object that represents an idea, place, or people. Flags can be symbols of a place, such as a country, or of a group of people, such as members of a sports club. When flags are symbols, they are much more than fluttering pieces of cloth. If someone chooses to hoist or wave a flag, it may be a source of great pride and a sign of that person's history, beliefs, or hopes.

Athletes proudly wave the flags of their countries at the Olympic Games. If fans are watching on television at home, a flag lets them pick out their national team and cheer them on.

National flags fly outside the United Nations headquarters in New York, in the United States.

An international organization that works for peace, the United Nations recognizes 195 countries.

Signals

For thousands of years, flags have been used as signals. A large, clear design makes them easy to recognize from a distance. A red flag is a common symbol of danger, while a white flag may be a sign of surrender. In many sports, flags are used to send messages—perhaps that a point has been scored—to players, umpires, or spectators. Differently patterned or positioned flags can also pass on complex information, from one ship to another or one mountaintop to another.

A flag on South Africa's Muizenberg Beach passes on a clear warning about the possibility of sharks in the water.

DID YOU KNOW? Some countries are not recognized as independent, separate states by the United Nations, but their flags are still sources of pride to those who fly them.

The Earliest Flags

There were flags for thousands of years before there were countries with carefully measured and agreed borders. Historians think the first flags were flown by armies. The earliest flags did not look like the square or rectangular cloth flags we usually fly today.

On the Battlefield

The earliest flag-like objects were held on poles, called battle standards, so soldiers could spot their own side on the battlefield. We know from artworks that, as early as 3000 BCE, ancient Egyptian armies were carrying staffs decorated with ornaments such as ostrich feathers. Other early battle standards were made of metal or of animal fur or tails. In the chaos of hand-to-hand fighting, a symbol held high above the crowd created a location to reach when new orders were needed or a retreat was taking place. Soldiers were encouraged to take pride in the symbols of their side, such as the eagles on the standards of the Roman army or the dragon-headed, kite-like standards of the Sarmatians. The sight of these symbols, and the fear that defeat would result in them being stolen by the enemy, spurred on soldiers to greater bravery.

This painted casket in the tomb of Egyptian Pharaoh Tutankhamun (c.1341–1323 BCE) shows soldiers carrying staffs decorated with feathers.

FLAG FOCUS: Derafsh Kaviani

Type: Empire

In use: c.224–651 CE

Flown by: The Sasanian Empire, centered on the region of modern Iran

Design: Derafsh Kaviani means "Standard of the Kings." Descriptions tell us the flag featured a large star on a purple background. The star represented good fortune, so loss or damage of the standard on the battlefield was expected to bring defeat. The flag was studded with jewels. Its edges had trailing streamers or fringes in red, gold, and purple.

The Bayeux Tapestry shows the Battle of Hastings, fought between the Normans and English in 1066 CE.

An English foot soldier holds a pennon flag, with forked tongues, attached to a spear.

The Vexillum

The study of flags is called vexillology. This word comes from the *vexillum*, a battle standard used by the armies of ancient Rome. The word *vexillum* itself comes from the Latin for "sail." The *vexillum* was not the first cloth flag, which was probably flown in ancient India or China, but it was an early and well-known example of a flag that was both cloth and four-sided. Unlike most modern flags, which fly from a vertical pole, the *vexillum* was hung from a horizontal pole that joined to a vertical staff. Each military unit, or organized group of soldiers, had its own *vexillum* decorated with words or symbols.

This carving in honor of the Roman Emperor Trajan (53–117 CE) shows two fringed *vexilla* (plural of *vexillum*).

DID YOU KNOW? One of the oldest flags ever found is the Shahdad Standard, which was made of bronze in the region of Iran in around 2400 BCE.

Heraldry

Heraldry is the design and study of coats of arms, badges, and mottoes that are symbols of families or other groups. Heraldry developed in the Middle Ages, when helmeted knights used these symbols on shields and banners to show their identity on the battlefield. Many modern flags display coats of arms that were first seen in battle.

Coats of Arms

The word "heraldry" comes from the officers, called heralds, employed by European kings and lords to keep track of the designs used by the noble knights who fought for them. The designs became symbols of a family's honor and were passed down the generations. Devices were later created for towns, organizations, and countries. The key element of a heraldic device is a coat of arms in the shape of a shield. Alongside the shield are often "supporters," which are animals or people that appear to hold it up. Above the shield may be a helmet bearing a crest, at first based on those worn by knights but soon too elaborate to be on a battlefield. Another feature is a motto, a short phrase expressing intentions or character.

The heraldic design of the British royal family features a quartered shield, depicting in two quarters the three lions *passant* (walking) of England, in another the lion *rampant* (standing on back legs) of Scotland, and in the fourth a harp for Ireland. The crest is a lion *statant* (on four legs) wearing a crown. The left supporter is a crowned English lion, while the right is a Scottish unicorn. The motto *"Dieu et mon droit"* is French for "God and my right," referring to the belief of medieval kings that they had a God–given right to rule.

This fully armed samurai has a banner showing his *mon*.

Samurai

In the Middle Ages, Japan developed its own system of heraldry similar to those of Europe. It developed on battlefields among the warriors of wealthy families, known as samurai. A *mon* was the emblem used to identify a family. Most *mons* were round and depicted a simplified animal, plant, object, or geometric shape.

DID YOU KNOW? Designed in 1971, the coat of arms of the Bahamas, in the Caribbean, is supported by a flamingo and a large fish known as a marlin.

The Church of St Mark, in Croatia's Zagreb, displays the coat of arms of the old Kingdom of Croatia-Slavonia.

The coat of arms of Zagreb is a white, three-towered city with a star and a crescent moon.

FLAG FOCUS:
Madrid

Type: City

In use: 1967–present

Flown by: Madrid, the capital of Spain

Design: The crimson flag features the city's coat of arms, which has shown a bear eating the fruits of a strawberry tree since 1222. It is believed the bear represents the people of Madrid and their medieval rights to pick forest fruits. The stars around the shield's borders represent the brightest stars in the Great Bear constellation.

Maritime Flags

For centuries, flags have been vital at sea for displaying the nationality of a ship, as well as the intentions—peaceful or warlike—of its captain. Although today's captains can communicate by radio, maritime flags are still crucial to identify ships from a distance. The rules about the flying of maritime flags must be followed strictly.

Ensigns

An ensign is a national flag, often different from the country's usual flag, flown on a ship to show its country. The ensign is usually flown at the stern (rear) of the ship while in port and may be moved to a mast in the middle of the ship when under way. Countries may have different ensigns for navy ships, merchant ships, and yachts sailed for pleasure. When a merchant ship enters waters belonging to another country, it must display a smaller ensign of that country, on a different mast, to show its intentions are friendly. Merchant ships dip their ensigns to salute passing warships. During wartime, ships lower their ensign if they are surrendering.

This steamboat is on Lake Geneva, which is shared between Switzerland and France, so it flies the French flag from its prow.

A South Korean navy ship flies its ensign, which features the same circular *taegeuk* symbol (see page 50) as the national flag, placed on crossed anchors.

FLAG FOCUS:
Bolivian Naval Ensign

Type: Naval ensign

In use: 2013–present

Flown by: Ships of the Bolivian navy

Design: This flag has a dark blue background, representing the country's waters. In the top left corner are two squares featuring: on the left, the stripes of the national flag; and on the right, the Wiphala, a rainbow-squared banner representing the country's indigenous peoples. The nine small stars represent the country's nine regions.

Pirate Flags

Pirates have sailed the oceans from the earliest days of sea travel to the present. They were particularly common during a period known as the Golden Age of Piracy, lasting from around 1650 to 1750. During this time, pirates flew special flags, often known as Jolly Rogers, when they were about to attack. At other times, they avoided notice by flying no flag or the flag of a friendly country. Jolly Rogers were meant to terrify the crew of another ship into surrendering. One frequently used design featured a white skull and crossbones on a black background.

The name Jolly Roger may come from the French *Joli Rouge* (Pretty Red), a red flag used by French pirates.

LA SUISSE

Since the boat is Swiss, it flies the ensign of Switzerland at its stern.

DID YOU KNOW? If a ship flies two ensigns on the same mast, it means the ship has been captured, with the upper ensign belonging to the captor.

Flag Signals

On beaches, railroads, and ships—and in emergencies of all kinds—flags are used as a way of communicating. Sometimes, it is a flag's color or design that gives important information. In the flag semaphore system, it is the positions of two flags that spell out messages.

Swimming Flags

On many beaches around the world, flags are used by lifeguards to signal if the water is safe. Although the colors of the flags used differ a little around the world, a red flag often shows that the water is extremely unsafe for swimming; yellow signifies difficult swimming conditions, such as a strong current; and green shows that the water is safe for swimming, as long as care is taken.

In many countries, lifeguards mark the limits of the area they are watching using a red and yellow flag.

In Thailand, a railroad signalman raises a green flag.

FLAG FOCUS: Affirmative

Type: International Code of Signals

In use: 1965–present

Flown by: Ships that need to communicate important information about safety

Design: This striped blue, red, and white flag is part of the International Code of Signals made up of 40 flags. This flag means both "Yes" and "C." When used in combination with other flags, it can also mean "I am abandoning ship" and "I need help."

DID YOU KNOW? In 2020, during the COVID–19 pandemic, people in Malaysia flew a white flag outside their home if they were in need of food or help.

Semaphore

One of the earliest semaphore systems was developed in France in 1792, using lines of towers, spaced several miles apart, with two arms that could be moved into different positions. This enabled messages to be passed along, over long distances, on land. A similar system, using a pair of flags, was adopted on board ships. Today, semaphore is still sometimes used by sailors, mountaineers, police officers, lifeguards, and Scouts.

A–1	B–2	C–3	D–4	E–5	F–6
G–7	H–8	I–9	J–0	K	L
M	N	O	P	Q	R
S	T	U	V	W	X
Y	Z	NUMERALS	ERROR/ATTENTION	CANCEL/ANNUL	REST/SPACE

Sporting Flags

Flags are used in sports from soccer to hurling, to indicate that a point has been scored or a rule has been broken. In some sports, such as the rodeo event of flag racing and the foot sport of capture the flag, it is flags themselves that are the object of the game—the first to grab a flag and complete the course is the winner!

Playing by the Rules

In soccer, American and Canadian football, and lacrosse, officials use flags to signal events including a rule being broken, such as by fouling, or the ball going out of play. In soccer, flags are waved by an assistant referee, while in the other sports it is wrapped around a weight so it can be thrown, usually to the spot where the rule was broken, without being blown away. In Australian rules football, Gaelic football, and hurling (in which balls are hit with sticks called hurleys), flags of different colors are waved to indicate a goal or point. Yacht racing and motor racing use a variety of flags to pass on information to racers as they speed past.

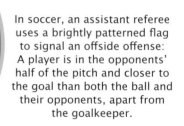

In soccer, an assistant referee uses a brightly patterned flag to signal an offside offense: A player is in the opponents' half of the pitch and closer to the goal than both the ball and their opponents, apart from the goalkeeper.

Flag Throwing

The sport of flag throwing is practiced in some Italian towns to mark festivals. The flag throwers (*sbandieratori*) toss the flags into the air so that they twist and twirl without touching the ground, with points usually awarded for the most elaborate throws. The flags belong to the town's different districts or guilds (groups of workers). The sport began in the Middle Ages as a competition between guilds.

Sbandieratori compete in Volterra, Italy, just as they first did in 1406.

FLAG FOCUS: Code 60

Type: International Automobile Federation (FIA)

In use: 2011–present

Flown by: FIA motor race officials in races such as the 24 Hours of Le Mans

Design: This pink flag with "60" at its center indicates that a Code 60 period is starting: Drivers must slow their cars to a maximum of 60 km/h (37 mph) and not overtake any other car. The flag is waved when there is bad weather or an obstruction on the track, as an alternative to stopping the race entirely.

In motor racing, a checkered flag is waved as the lead driver passes the finish line.

Racing driver Max Verstappen wins the Formula One Austrian Grand Prix.

DID YOU KNOW? Flags mark the holes in golf, with different colors sometimes used to show the hole's position on the green, the area of trimmed grass around the hole.

15

Religious Flags

Several of the world's religions are represented by a flag, such as the five-colored flag of Jainism and the red cross on blue and white of the Christian flag. In addition, many national flags use symbols to represent the religion of the majority of their citizens, such as the Star of David of Judaism, cross of Christianity, and crescent moon of Islam.

Tibetan Prayer Flags

In Tibet, Buddhists hang prayer flags in high places, between mountain peaks and rooftops. Buddhists follow the teachings of Guatama Buddha, who lived in India in the 5th–4th century BCE. The flags are in one of five colors that represent five elements: blue (sky and space), white (air and wind), red (fire), green (water), and yellow (earth). They are printed with prayers and mantras (religious sayings). The prayers are not for personal hopes, but are believed to be blown by the wind to spread peace, kindness, and love through the universe.

Tibetans constantly place new prayer flags beside old ones, as a recognition of the cycle of life, from birth to death to birth.

FLAG FOCUS: Buddhist

Type: Religion

In use: 1885–present

Flown by: Buddhists across the world

Design: The flag's six vertical bands represent the colors of the aura (light) given off by the Buddha when he gained Enlightenment (true wisdom): blue (representing compassion), yellow (finding a path between extremes), red (goodness), white (purity), orange (wisdom), and a combination of the other colors, representing eternal truths.

DID YOU KNOW? Crosses, representing the cross on which Christ died, are featured on 28 of the world's country flags.

The Nishan Sahib

The Nishan Sahib ("Exalted Ensign") is the flag of Sikhism, a religion that grew up in the Punjab region of India in the 15th century. The saffron-colored triangular flag has a tassel at the tip and is marked with a black emblem known as a *khanda*, a symbol of Sikhism. It contains a *khanda* (double-edged sword) in the center, representing the ability of truth to cut through falsehood; a circle, representing unity and eternity; and two crossed *kirpans* (single-edged swords), signifying balance between the spirit and practical needs.

Banners proclaim their holders' faith in Christ and the Catholic Church.

The Nishan Sahib is carried during festival processions and hung on a tall flagpole outside *gurdwaras*, places of worship and meeting for Sikhs.

Flag Rules

Every country has rules around the use, raising, lowering, and disposal of its national flag. In some countries, these rules are just guidelines, while in many others—from Algeria to Zimbabwe—the rules are laid down by laws. Occasionally, breaking the law is punished by fines or even imprisonment.

Australian national flags are flown at half-mast on ANZAC day, when those who have died in wars are remembered.

Raising

All countries follow guidelines on how the national flag should be displayed alongside the flags of other countries, during visits by the government of other nations. The country's own flag usually takes the position of honor. It is flown on the left, with the flags of other countries following in alphabetical order in the language of the host country. The flag of an independent country should never be flown on the same flagpole or lower than the flag of another. When a country has suffered a great loss, such as a natural disaster, it is usual to fly the national flag below the top of its flagpole, called half-mast or half-staff.

Disposal

When a national flag becomes faded or ripped, all countries agree that it should no longer be flown. Many countries have rules about how to dispose of a worn flag. Some, such as Australia, state that it should be cut into small pieces so it is no longer recognizable (and no longer a symbol of the country's honor) and thrown away in a sealed bag. Many countries, including India, New Zealand, and the United States, ask that national flags be burned respectfully. Across the world, the burning of any national flag at other times is either deeply frowned on or forbidden by law.

In the United States, Boy Scouts (pictured), Girl Scouts, American Legions, and Veterans of Foreign Wars collect national flags and hold retirement ceremonies.

DID YOU KNOW? The flag of Saudi Arabia is never flown at half-mast because it bears an Islamic oath, so lowering it would be a sign of disrespect to God.

Type: State

In use: 1950–present

Flown by: The German government and navy ships

Design: Like many countries, Germany has variant flags, which are official national flags flown for different purposes. This flag is the state flag (flown by the government), as well as the naval ensign. It is the same as the civil flag flown by individuals and businesses, with the addition of a shield bearing a black eagle with red beak and claws.

Many countries have national days, when people are encouraged to fly the national flag.

France's national day is July 14, remembering the day in 1789 when the French Revolution began.

Flagpoles

Flags can be grasped in the hands or waved on short sticks, but most permanent flags are flown on tall flagpoles made of wood or metal. Flags are attached to a rope that runs round a circular wheel, called a pulley, at the top of the pole, so the other end of the rope can be pulled to hoist the flag. The top of the pole is usually decorated by a ball or flat plate known as a "truck."

Dhwaja Stambha

A Dhwaja Stambha (from the Sanskrit for "flagpole") stands outside many Hindu temples. It is usually covered in a metal such as silver, copper, or brass. At the top, the flagpole has three horizontal branches pointing toward the temple's sanctum, an innermost area where a statue of the temple's primary god is kept. The three branches symbolize the three gods Vishnu, Brahma, and Shiva, the key forms of Brahman, source of all life. During festivals, the Dhwaja Stambha is adorned with flags.

The Dhwaja Stambha is seen as a link between earth and heaven.

It is 561 ft (171 m) high and constructed from 550 US tons (500 tonnes) of steel.

FLAG FOCUS: Mars

Type: Planet

In use: Not in official use

Flown by: Scientists who are members of the Mars Society

Design: This is one of several flags designed for Mars, which may be put in use if humans ever land on the planet and set up home. It was designed by Pascal Lee, an engineer at the National Aeronautics and Space Administration (NASA), in 1999. Its three colors represent the planet's possible transformation from a lifeless, dry planet with reddish soil to one with plants (green) and water (blue).

The Lunar Flag Assembly

When the United States landed the first humans on the moon in 1969, the astronauts planted their national flag on its surface. The flagpole they used had been specially designed. Since there is little atmosphere on the moon, the flag could not flutter in the wind, which would make it look disappointing in photographs. To solve this problem, the Lunar Flag Assembly was designed with a horizontal bar at its top. The flag was a standard government flag sewn to create a pocket for the horizontal bar. In their heavy suits, the astronauts found the vertical pole difficult to press into the moon's dust, resulting in the flag falling over from the force of their takeoff when they returned home.

The world's tallest flagpole was erected in Jeddah, Saudi Arabia, in 2014.

On July 21, 1969, the second human on the moon, Buzz Aldrin, admires the Lunar Flag Assembly, in a photo taken by the first human on the moon, Neil Armstrong.

DID YOU KNOW? When Edmund Hillary and Tenzing Norgay were the first to climb Mount Everest in 1953, they flew Nepalese, United Kingdom, and United Nations flags from an ax.

21

Flag Designs

Flags are dyed or stitched with a bold pattern that is easy to recognize and different from any other flag. The design may be modern, created by an artist or politician, or based on ancient symbols of the country's rulers, religion, or animals. Flags are usually rectangular, but may also be square, triangular, or swallowtailed (with a V-shaped cut, creating "tails").

Proportions and Parts

The proportion of a flag is the relationship between its vertical height and its horizontal width. A square flag is 1:1. The only national flag with a width more than twice its height is the flag of Qatar, with a proportion of 11:28 (if its height were 11 m, its width would be 28 m). Vexillologists use special terms to describe the parts of a flag:

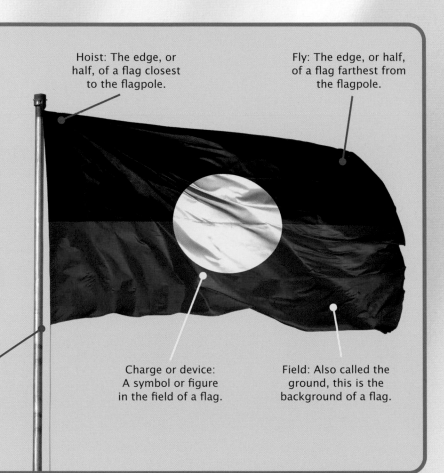

Hoist: The edge, or half, of a flag closest to the flagpole.

Fly: The edge, or half, of a flag farthest from the flagpole.

Charge or device: A symbol or figure in the field of a flag.

Field: Also called the ground, this is the background of a flag.

Adopted in 1995, the Australian Aboriginal flag has a field divided into equal horizontal stripes of black and red, making it a bicolor (two-color) flag. It is charged with a yellow disk, representing the sun. The flag has a proportion of 1:2, which means its vertical height is half its horizontal width.

FLAG FOCUS: Sükhbaatar

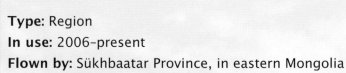

Type: Region

In use: 2006–present

Flown by: Sükhbaatar Province, in eastern Mongolia

Design: This flag has a light blue fess on a red field. Its charge is the province's coat of arms, featuring a winged horse and the name of the province in Cyrillic and Mongol scripts. The flag has a proportion of 3:7 and has three tails on the fly, made from two identical cut-outs composed of a disk and intersecting triangle.

Common Flag Designs

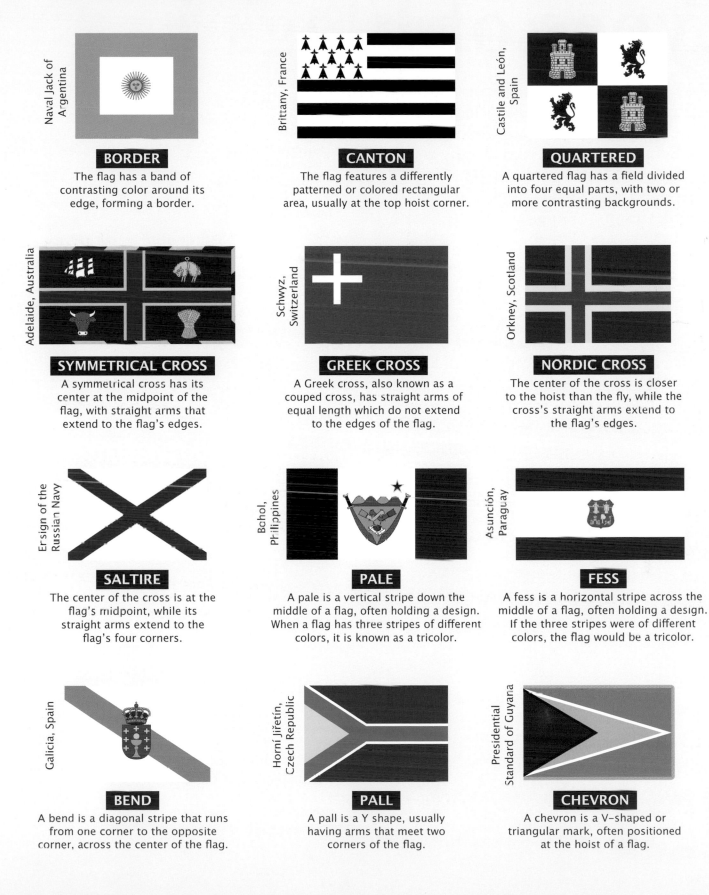

Naval Jack of Argentina

BORDER

The flag has a band of contrasting color around its edge, forming a border.

Brittany, France

CANTON

The flag features a differently patterned or colored rectangular area, usually at the top hoist corner.

Castile and León, Spain

QUARTERED

A quartered flag has a field divided into four equal parts, with two or more contrasting backgrounds.

Adelaide, Australia

SYMMETRICAL CROSS

A symmetrical cross has its center at the midpoint of the flag, with straight arms that extend to the flag's edges.

Schwyz, Switzerland

GREEK CROSS

A Greek cross, also known as a couped cross, has straight arms of equal length which do not extend to the edges of the flag.

Orkney, Scotland

NORDIC CROSS

The center of the cross is closer to the hoist than the fly, while the cross's straight arms extend to the flag's edges.

Ensign of the Russian Navy

SALTIRE

The center of the cross is at the flag's midpoint, while its straight arms extend to the flag's four corners.

Bohol, Philippines

PALE

A pale is a vertical stripe down the middle of a flag, often holding a design. When a flag has three stripes of different colors, it is known as a tricolor.

Asunción, Paraguay

FESS

A fess is a horizontal stripe across the middle of a flag, often holding a design. If the three stripes were of different colors, the flag would be a tricolor.

Galicia, Spain

BEND

A bend is a diagonal stripe that runs from one corner to the opposite corner, across the center of the flag.

Horní Jiřetín, Czech Republic

PALL

A pall is a Y shape, usually having arms that meet two corners of the flag.

Presidential Standard of Guyana

CHEVRON

A chevron is a V–shaped or triangular mark, often positioned at the hoist of a flag.

DID YOU KNOW? Only four national flags have a border: Grenada, Maldives, Montenegro, and Sri Lanka.

Types of Flags

There are many different types of flags, including national, regional, and city flags. In addition, flags represent clubs, businesses, schools, and colleges. Sometimes people who identify as having the same ethnicity, sexuality, or culture design a flag to symbolize their shared pride, history, or hopes.

Although the Republic of Venice fell in 1797, its flag is flown in the city of Venice today.

Places

Although flags were flown to represent rulers and their armies for thousands of years, the idea of having a flag to represent a country off the battlefield did not fully take shape until the 17th century. Countries started to adopt flag designs by law. These designs were often based on existing battle standards or the personal flags of the ruler. Today, every country has a national flag, which may have variants for the use of the government, president, armed forces, and ordinary citizens. Different regions or cities within a country may also fly their own flags, usually alongside or below the national flag. In addition, most overseas territories (such as the United States' Guam) and constituent countries (such as New Zealand's Cook Islands) fly their own designs.

In Japan, the flag of Shisuoka Prefecture (right) flies beside the national flag. The Shisuoka flag is charged with an emblem that both looks like the region's Mount Fuji volcano and is a simplified map of the prefecture itself.

FLAG FOCUS: Johannesburg

Type: City

In use: 1997–present

Flown by: Johannesburg, the largest city in South Africa

Design: Using the colors of the national flag, this city's flag is a vertical tricolor of blue, green, and red, with white fimbriations (narrow stripes in a contrasting color). In the pale is the coat of arms of Johannesburg, consisting of a green warrior's shield, supported by two young lions with beaded collars.

Organizations

The first organizations to design their own flags were probably the guilds of medieval Europe. These organizations represented craftspeople or merchants. Their flags usually advertised their members' goods, with perhaps the guild of wool sellers showing a sheep and the guild of stonemasons a chisel. Over the centuries, countless groups have adopted flags, including political parties, sporting teams, and charities.

The flag of Futbal Club Barcelona displays the team's colors and crest, which contains a soccer tball.

The flag has six rectangular tails and is charged with the Lion of Saint Mark, representing the city's patron saint.

DID YOU KNOW? Like the flag of India, the flag of the Romani people features a wheel of dharma ("law"), which represents their traditional traveling lifestyle.

International Flags

A few flags are recognized across the world as symbols of safety, progress, or togetherness. Some belong to intergovernmental organizations, which are groups of governments that work together toward common goals. Others represent charities that help people wherever they are needed.

The Red Cross

One of the first widely recognized international flags was that of the Red Cross, an organization founded in 1863 to help people wounded in wars. The organization needed a bold flag that would be easily spotted in chaotic and frightening situations. Its Swiss founders, Henry Dunant and Gustave Moynier, decided to use the Swiss flag, with its colors reversed: a red cross on a white field. Today, the organization also has two other flags, as crosses are associated with Christianity: a Red Crescent, used in Muslim regions, and a Red Crystal, associated with no religion.

The United Nations flag features a map of the world centered on the North Pole, surrounded by olive branches, which are international symbols of peace.

The International Red Cross and Red Crescent Movement works to protect human life and health.

DID YOU KNOW? Designed in 1913, the flag of the Olympic Games features five linked rings, representing five continents: Africa, America, Asia, Europe, and Oceania.

Type: International organization

In use: 2016–present

Flown by: The eight members of the Nordic Council, which represents countries and territories in northern Europe

Design: The flag features the simplified shape of a swan, in a white circle on a blue field. The swan symbolizes trust, honesty, and freedom. In Norse mythology, swans turned white because they drank from a well of pure and holy water. Finland's national bird is the whooper swan, while Denmark's is the mute swan.

The United Nations

The United Nations (UN) was founded after World War II (1939–45) to prevent future wars. Its members meet to discuss the world's issues, enforce international law, and agree action to prevent conflict and promote progress. The UN also sends peacekeepers to regions where conflict has recently stopped to make sure the terms of peace agreements are met. To be easily recognized, peacekeepers fly the UN flag.

The flag was based on a design created by American architect Donal McLaughlin.

The blue was chosen as the opposite of red, the color of war.

This version of the flag, with the outline of the United States at the center, was used between 1945 and 1947. It was then altered so no country seemed to be favored.

North Africa

Apart from Egypt, all of North Africa's countries have a five-pointed star on their flag. The five points represent the Five Pillars of Islam, which are the five acts central to the lives of Muslims. These are belief in God, prayer, giving to the needy, fasting during the holy month of Ramadan, and pilgrimage to the holy city of Mecca, in Saudi Arabia.

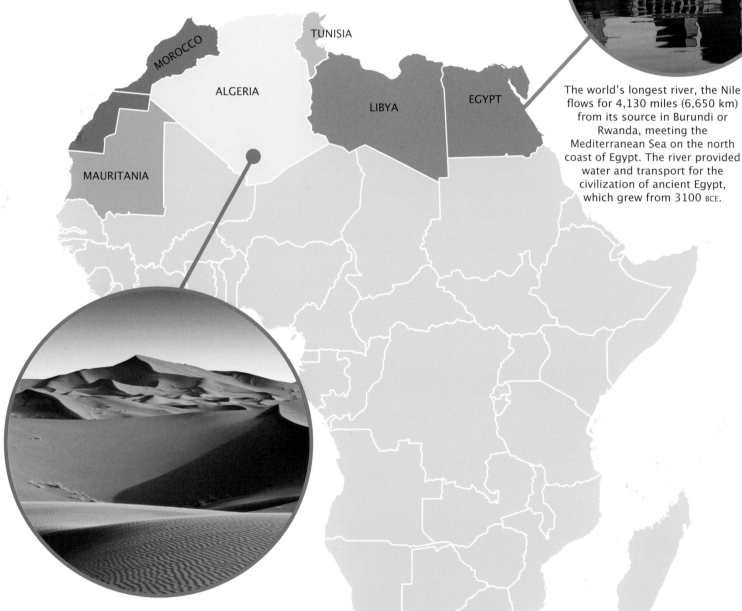

The world's longest river, the Nile flows for 4,130 miles (6,650 km) from its source in Burundi or Rwanda, meeting the Mediterranean Sea on the north coast of Egypt. The river provided water and transport for the civilization of ancient Egypt, which grew from 3100 BCE.

Covering 3.6 million sq miles (9.2 million sq km), the Sahara Desert is the world's biggest hot desert. On average, the Sahara's central region gets less than 0.04 in (1 mm) of rain per year. The desert's sands are represented on the flag of Mauritania.

MAURITANIA

On the flag of Mauritania, green represents Islam, the religion of the majority of the nation's people. Yellow represents the sands of the Sahara Desert, which covers 90 percent of the country's land. The red bands represent the Mauritanian people's willingness to defend their country with their blood. In combination, green, yellow, and red are the Pan-African colors (see page 32). The central crescent and star are symbols of Islam (see page 30).

MOROCCO

Adopted in 1915, the Moroccan flag features a green interlaced star emblazoned on a red field. In addition to the Five Pillars of Islam, the five points of the star stand for love, truth, peace, freedom, and justice. A variant flag of Morocco has a gold, one-starred crown in the top left corner, representing the King of Morocco, who acts as a figurehead, or symbolic leader, of the country, which is governed by an elected parliament.

ALGERIA

The flag of Algeria has two equal vertical bands of green and white. White represents peace while green represents Islam. Centered on the dividing line is a red crescent moon encircling a red star, a symbol of the nation's main religion, Islam (see page 30). The crescent is more closed than those of other regional flags, representing a desire to grasp happiness. The flag was adopted in 1962, when Algeria gained independence from France.

TUNISIA

Tunisia's flag has a red field with a centered white disk, representing the sun and suggesting the nation's shining achievements and bright future. Inside the disk is a red crescent and five-pointed star, representing Islam (see page 30). Red represents resistance to invasion, while white symbolizes peace. A variant flag, used by the president, also bears the words "For the Nation" written in Arabic.

LIBYA

Unlike the other flags in this region, the flag of Libya has a proportion of 1:2, which means its width is twice its height. The flag was adopted in 1951, fell out of use in 1969, then was readopted in 2011. The central black stripe is double the height of the red and green stripes. The flag's colors represent different regions of the country: red for Fezzan, black for Cyrenaica, and green for Tripolitania.

EGYPT

Egypt's flag uses the same horizontal tricolor of red, white, and black as the flags of Iraq, Syria, Sudan, and Yemen. These are the colors of Arab Liberation, first flown during the 1952 Egyptian Revolution, when the Egyptians overthrew their king and fought for freedom from British occupation. This was the beginning of a wave of revolutions against foreign rule by Arabic-speaking nations across North Africa and the Middle East.

DID YOU KNOW? Although many country flags feature five-pointed stars, only Morocco's and Ethiopia's have an open (unfilled) star, known as a pentagram.

The Eagle of Saladin

The eagle at the center of Egypt's flag is known as the Eagle of Saladin. The first sultan of Egypt and Syria, Saladin (1137–93) fought against Christian knights, known as Crusaders, who seized land in the Middle East. Saladin's personal flag featured a red eagle, a symbol of strength. Saladin and his people could see eagles and other birds of prey in the carvings and paintings of ancient Egyptian temples. The ancient goddess Nekhbet was often shown as a vulture or eagle, her wings stretched protectively to keep Egypt safe. Today, the Eagle of Saladin is a symbol of unity among Arab countries. It also appears on the coats of arms, although not the flags, of Iraq and Palestine.

This painting of Nekhbet is in the temple of ancient Egypt's Queen Hatshepsut.

The Star and Crescent Moon

In North Africa, the flags of Algeria, Libya, Mauritania, and Tunisia all feature a star and crescent moon. A crescent with one or more stars also appears on the flags of Azerbaijan, Comoros, Croatia, Malaysia, Singapore, Turkey, Turkmenistan, Pakistan, and Uzbekistan. In all these countries except Croatia (see page 81) and Singapore (see page 57), the majority of people are Muslims. The star and crescent is often seen as a symbol of Islam. From the 18th century, the symbol was used on flags of the Ottoman Empire, a powerful Muslim state that ruled a vast region including Algeria, Libya, Tunisia, and Turkey.

A crescent moon is often seen on the roofs of mosques, where Muslims pray and worship.

DID YOU KNOW? Mauritania flies the world's newest national flag, which was redesigned to include its horizontal red bands in 2017.

Red is the color of Morocco's royal family, the Alaouites.

In Islam, green is the color of heavenly paradise.

FLAG FOCUS:
Arab League

Type: International organization

In use: 1945–present

Flown by: 22 Arabic-speaking countries in North Africa and the Middle East that are members of the Arab League

Design: A yellow chain with 22 links represents the 22 members of the league, while two olive branches represent peace. Within a crescent moon, the name of the organization is written in Arabic. The green of the background is one of the Pan-Arab colors (see page 37) and also represents Islam.

West Africa

Several countries in this region, and many on the rest of the continent, fly flags featuring the Pan-African colors: green, yellow, and red. This color combination was first used by Ethiopia (see page 37). After gaining independence from European rule, many countries—starting with Ghana in 1957—adopted these colors out of respect for the fact that Ethiopia was only briefly conquered. The colors stand for the unity of African peoples.

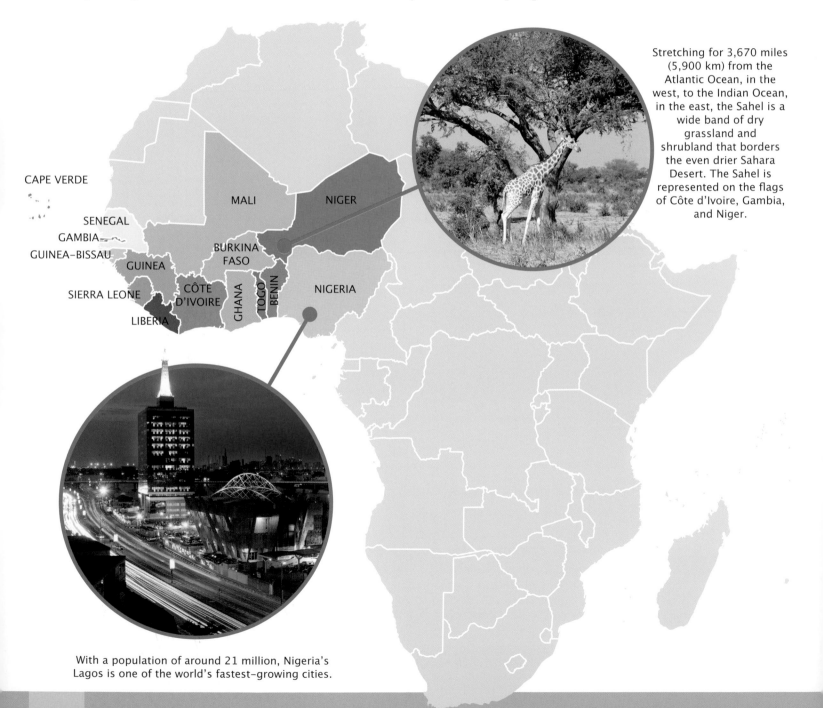

CAPE VERDE

SENEGAL

GAMBIA

GUINEA-BISSAU

GUINEA

SIERRA LEONE

LIBERIA

MALI

BURKINA FASO

CÔTE D'IVOIRE

GHANA

TOGO

BENIN

NIGER

NIGERIA

Stretching for 3,670 miles (5,900 km) from the Atlantic Ocean, in the west, to the Indian Ocean, in the east, the Sahel is a wide band of dry grassland and shrubland that borders the even drier Sahara Desert. The Sahel is represented on the flags of Côte d'Ivoire, Gambia, and Niger.

With a population of around 21 million, Nigeria's Lagos is one of the world's fastest-growing cities.

CAPE VERDE

In the flag of the islands of Cape Verde, the blue field represents sea and sky. Stripes of white and red represent the "road" of progress. A circle of ten stars (see page 35) are centered on the road.

SENEGAL

This tricolor of the Pan-African colors bears a green star at its center. For the nation's Muslims, the green of the star represents Islam, while for all Senegalese it suggests hope and growth.

GAMBIA

Adopted in 1965, Gambia's flag has stripes of red (representing the Sahel), blue (symbolizing the Gambia River), green (standing for the coastal forests), and white (representing unity).

GUINEA-BISSAU

Influenced by the flag of Ghana, the 1973 flag of Guinea-Bissau displays the Pan-African colors, which also represent blood (red), wealth (yellow), and the country's forests (green).

GUINEA

In use since 1958, the flag of Guinea is a tricolor of the Pan-African colors, used in a reverse order to the flag of Mali. Like many flags in the region, this flag's proportions are 2:3.

SIERRA LEONE

Adopted in 1961, when the country gained independence from the United Kingdom, the flag has equal horizontal stripes of green (representing farming), white (for unity), and blue (for the ocean).

LIBERIA

With an unusual proportion of 10:19 (making it almost twice as wide as it is high), this flag has six red stripes, five white stripes, and a white five-pointed star on a blue square in its upper left canton.

MALI

This flag was adopted in 1961, shortly after Mali won independence from France. The Pan-African colors also represent growth (green), wealth (yellow), and the fight for independence (red).

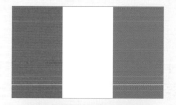

CÔTE D'IVOIRE

In this 1959 flag, orange represents the soil and the dry plants of the northern Sahel, white stands for peace, and green represents both hope and the green forests of the Atlantic Coast.

BURKINA FASO

Using the Pan-African colors, the flag of Burkina Faso is emblazoned with a five-pointed star that represents truth and justice. The flag was adopted in 1984.

GHANA

The flag of Ghana was designed by artist and hockey player Theodosia Okoh in 1957. Red represents love, yellow is for the country's gold, and green is for its farms and forests.

TOGO

The Togo flag has an unusual proportion of 1:1.618034, a ratio—known as the golden ratio—that is believed to be pleasing to look at. It was designed by artist Paul Ahyi in 1960.

BENIN

For Benin, the Pan-African colors also represent hope (green), the courage of its people past and present (red), and the nation's treasures (yellow). The three rectangles are all the same size.

NIGER

This flag has a proportion of 6:7, making it nearly square. Orange represents the Sahel of the north, while green symbolizes the southern forests. The orange circle represents the sun.

NIGERIA

In this triband, green stands for the country's forests and fields, while white is for peace and unity. The flag was first flown on October 1, 1960, the day Nigeria gained independence from the United Kingdom.

DID YOU KNOW? In 1959, Nigerian student Taiwo Akinkunmi was studying in London, England, when he won a competition to design a flag for Nigeria.

Type: Region

In use: 1935–present

Flown by: The Ashanti region, in southern Ghana

Design: While the yellow horizontal band stands for the region's gold mines, the green band represents its forests. At the center is the Golden Stool ("Sika' Dwa"), symbol of the Ashanti people and throne of Ashanti kings, who today act as local leaders. Each stool is carved from a single tree trunk, with a curving seat, and covered with gold.

The Côte d'Ivoire flag is similar to the Irish flag (see page 69), but the orange and green bands are reversed.

When Cote d'Ivoire sprinter Murielle Ahouré won a race at the 2018 World Indoor Championships, she borrowed an Irish flag and reversed it.

DID YOU KNOW? The flag of Liberia (1847) is the oldest national African flag, followed by the flag of Morocco (1915).

Many Stars

Stars appear on 69 national flags, not including all the flags that depict the sun, our nearest star. In West Africa, the flags of Burkina Faso, Cape Verde, Ghana, Guinea-Bissau, Liberia, Senegal, and Togo feature stars. Stars are guides by which we can navigate at night. From ancient times, stars were often linked with the gods. The world's national flags use stars to symbolize hopes, ideals, people, or places. On the flag of Ghana, for example, the black star represents the freedom of Africa's people. Cape Verde's flag has 10 stars to represent the country's 10 main islands.

The 10 main islands of Cape Verde were formed by the eruption of hot rock, called lava, from the seafloor.

Liberia's Stars and Stripes

The flag of Liberia looks similar to the United States flag, known as the Stars and Stripes (see page 89). However, while the Stars and Stripes has 50 stars and 13 stripes, Liberia's flag has 1 star and 11 stripes. Liberia's flag was based on the United States flag because the country was founded by African Americans in the 19th century. They, or their ancestors, had been enslaved and taken to the United States or Caribbean. The 11 stripes symbolize the 11 people who signed Liberia's Declaration of Independence in 1847, making the country a self-governing nation.

Liberia's coat of arms celebrates the freedom gained by the African Americans who arrived in Liberia by ship.

East Africa

Many East African flags feature red, which represents the blood shed gaining independence from foreign rule. The oldest flag is Somalia's, which was designed in 1954. The newest belongs to South Sudan. Designed in 2005, this flag is older than its country, which did not gain independence from Sudan until 2011.

Known for its courtship dances and booming call, the gray crowned crane is the national bird of Uganda.

SUDAN

ERITREA

DJIBOUTI

ETHIOPIA

SOUTH SUDAN

SOMALIA

UGANDA

KENYA

RWANDA

BURUNDI

TANZANIA

At 19,341 ft (5,895 m) tall, snow-capped Mount Kilimanjaro is the highest mountain in Africa.

SUDAN

This flag features the Pan-Arab colors: black, white, green, and red. Each color represents an Arab dynasty (family)—the Abbasids, Umayyads, Fatimids, and Hashemites—who ruled the Middle East and North Africa.

ERITREA

The triangles on Eritrea's flag are green (for farming), red (for the blood shed during the fight for independence; see page 38), and blue (for ocean fishing). The red triangle is roughly the shape of the country.

SOUTH SUDAN

In this flag, black represents the people of South Sudan, red represents the struggle for independence, green represents the land, and blue stands for the River Nile, which waters the fields.

ETHIOPIA

Ethiopia's flag is a tricolor, a flag with three bands of different colors. The star at the center represents Ethiopia's bright future, while its equally spaced yellow rays represent the equality of all Ethiopians.

DJIBOUTI

In Djibouti's flag, pale blue represents the sea and sky, green represents the land, and white represents peace. The red star stands for unity, as well as the blood of those who fought for independence.

SOMALIA

The light blue of Somalia's flag stands for the sky and the ocean. The five-pointed white star represents the unity of Somalia's people. The flag was designed by Somali scholar Mohammed Awale Liban.

UGANDA

At the center of this flag is a gray crowned crane, its leg lifted to represent progress. The colors of the stripes are black (for Uganda's people), yellow (for the sun), and red (for shared blood).

KENYA

With a shield and spears (see page 38) at its center, this tricolor features black (for Kenya's people), red (for their blood), and green (for the land). White fimbriations (narrow stripes in a contrasting color) stand for peace.

RWANDA

Adopted in 2001, this flag has a sun in its top right corner, representing the education, openness, and unity of Rwanda's people. The flag's blue, yellow, and green stand for peace, development, and hope.

BURUNDI

Burundi's flag features a white saltire (diagonal cross; see page 26). The three stars represent the country's three main peoples—Hutu, Twa, and Tutsi—and the three parts of the national motto: "Unity, Work, and Progress."

TANZANIA

This flag was adopted in 1964 when the two states of Tanganyika and Zanzibar merged to form Tanzania. The flag incorporates the green of Tanganyika's flag and the blue of Zanzibar's, joined by a diagonal black band.

DID YOU KNOW? The horizontal stripes of the Ethiopian flag were originally red, yellow, then green, but the order was reversed in 1914.

A Warrior's Shield

Kenya and Eswatini (see page 45) are the only countries that have a traditional shield on their flag. In both flags, the shield symbolizes the defense of the country and its people. Kenya's flag shows a Maasai shield and two crossed spears. The Maasai live in Kenya and northern Tanzania. In the past, Maasai warriors used their spear and shield to defend themselves against enemies. Today, for those Maasai who lead a traditional lifestyle, spears are still a defense against lions and hyenas. A spear is also a prop to lean on while guarding a herd of goats or zebu, a type of cow.

A Maasai shield is made of zebu skin stretched over a wooden frame. Young warriors decorate their shields in black, gray, and white, while older men are allowed to add red to the pattern.

Olive Wreaths

The Eritrea flag features an olive wreath, the twigs bent into a ring. For thousands of years, an olive wreath has been a symbol of peace and victory. Olive wreaths were awarded to the winners in the ancient Olympic Games, which started in 776 BCE in Olympia, Greece. The wreath on Eritrea's flag has 30 leaves, to mark the 30 years, from 1961 to 1991, that the country fought for independence from Ethiopia. Inside the wreath is an olive branch with six leaves, representing the six regions of Eritrea. An olive wreath is also on the flags of Cyprus, Paraguay, Turkmenistan, the United Nations (see page 27), and the Arab League (see page 31).

At the 2004 Olympic Games in Athens, Greece, medal-winners were awarded olive wreaths, as in the ancient Olympics. Eritrea's Zersenay Tadese (right) won bronze in the 10,000-m race, while Ethiopia's Kenenisa Bekele won gold.

FLAG FOCUS:
East African Community

Type: International organization

In use: 2008–present

Flown by: Burundi, Kenya, Rwanda, South Sudan, Tanzania, and Uganda, which are members of the East African Community

Design: The blue stripes represent Lake Victoria (also shown in the central map), which lies in all the countries except South Sudan. The white, black, green, yellow, and red stripes are taken from the flags of the member countries. In the middle, a handshake represents trade and co-operation.

A Maasai spear has an iron, leaf-shaped blade and a long wooden shaft.

Traditionally, red dye is made of zebu blood mixed with earth and fruit sap.

DID YOU KNOW? The flags of South Sudan and Gambia use a blue stripe or triangle to represent their country's major river, which is vital to the nation for water and transport.

Central Africa

Six Central African flags feature green stripes. While green is one of the Pan-African colors, symbolizing African unity, the color also represents this region's vast forests. Central Africa's newest flag belongs to the Democratic Republic of the Congo, which adopted its current design in 2006. The oldest, belonging to the Central African Republic, was designed in 1958.

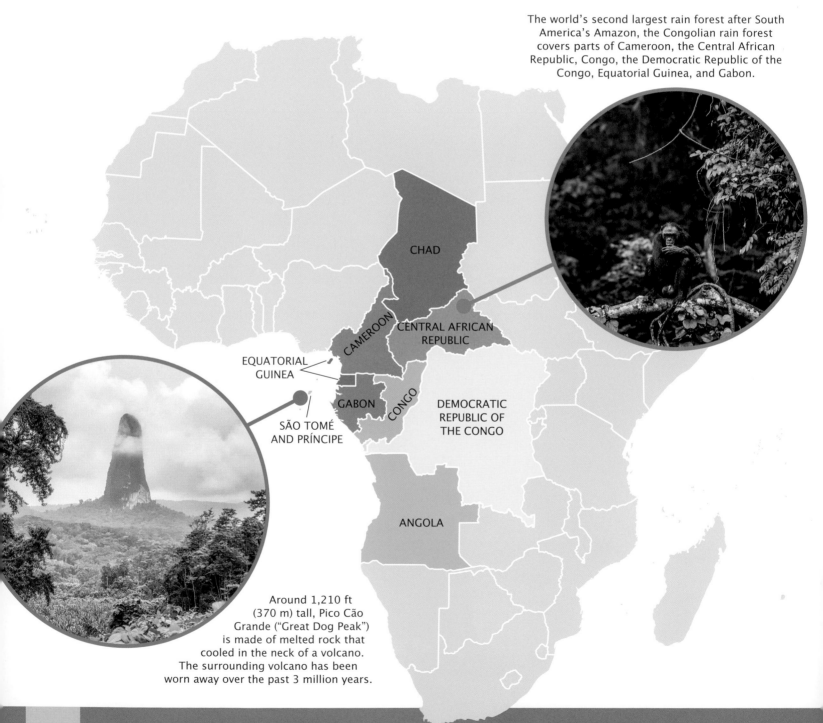

The world's second largest rain forest after South America's Amazon, the Congolian rain forest covers parts of Cameroon, the Central African Republic, Congo, the Democratic Republic of the Congo, Equatorial Guinea, and Gabon.

CHAD

CAMEROON

CENTRAL AFRICAN REPUBLIC

EQUATORIAL GUINEA

GABON

CONGO

DEMOCRATIC REPUBLIC OF THE CONGO

SÃO TOMÉ AND PRÍNCIPE

ANGOLA

Around 1,210 ft (370 m) tall, Pico Cão Grande ("Great Dog Peak") is made of melted rock that cooled in the neck of a volcano. The surrounding volcano has been worn away over the past 3 million years.

CHAD

The flag of Chad is a vertical tricolor of blue, yellow, and red. It was adopted in 1959. Reflecting the country's rule by France (1920-60), the design is similar to the French tricolor of blue, white, and red, but yellow—one of the Pan-African colors—replaces the white. In addition, the blue signifies hope, the yellow represents the sun and desert, and the red represents the blood shed for independence.

CAMEROON

A tricolor of the Pan-African colors, the flag of Cameroon is emblazoned with a yellow star. There is no standard size for the star, but it is always contained within the red stripe. The green stripe represents the forests of southern Cameroon, while yellow signifies the dry grasslands of the north. Red represents the unity of the Cameroonian people. The current design was adopted in 1975.

CENTRAL AFRICAN REPUBLIC

The blue, white, and red of this flag are taken from the flag of France, which ruled this region until 1960. The red, green, and yellow are the Pan-African colors. The red stripe ties together past and future, as well as signifying the respect that people of all nations should have for each other. The flag was adopted in 1958.

EQUATORIAL GUINEA

This horizontal tricolor of green, white, and red has a blue isosceles triangle (with two equal sides) at its hoist. At the flag's center is the national coat of arms, consisting of a shield decorated with a silk cotton tree (see page 42), six six-pointed stars (representing the mainland and five major islands), and the national motto: *Unidad, Paz, Justicia* (Unity, Peace, Justice).

SÃO TOMÉ AND PRÍNCIPE

In the flag of São Tomé and Príncipe, the green stripes represent the country's lush plant life, while the yellow stripe signifies the hot sun and the country's key crop, cocoa. The red isosceles triangle represents the struggle for independence from Portugal, which was won in 1975. The two black stars stand for the country's two main islands, which lie in the Atlantic Ocean.

GABON

With a proportion of 3:4, the flag of Gabon is nearly as tall as it is wide. This unusual proportion is shared only with the national flags of Democratic Republic of the Congo, Papua New Guinea, and San Marino. The yellow stripe represents the equator, which runs through Gabon. The green stripe stands for Gabon's forests, while the blue signifies the Atlantic Ocean.

CONGO

A yellow diagonal band divides the Congo flag into triangles of green and red. This is the only flag using the Pan-African colors which has a diagonal stripe in its design. The green symbolizes the country's forests and farms, while yellow represents friendship. Some say that the red represents the struggle for independence, which was gained in 1960.

DEMOCRATIC REPUBLIC OF THE CONGO

A sky blue field is cut diagonally by a red band with yellow fimbriations. A yellow five-pointed star, representing a bright future, is in the upper left canton. The blue represents peace, the red stands for the blood of those who fought for their country, and the yellow is for the nation's wealth. The current flag is similar to one flown between 1963 and 1971.

ANGOLA

The Angolan flag was adopted in 1975, replacing the flag of Portugal, which was flown in Angola during the time it was ruled by Portugal. The flag has two horizontal bands, of red (signifying the blood shed in defense of the country) and black (representing Africa). At the center of the flag is a gear and machete emblem, crowned with a star (see page 42).

DID YOU KNOW? The flag of Chad is identical to the flag of Romania (see page 85), although Chad's flag allows its color range to vary a little.

The Silk Cotton Tree

On a shield at the center of the Equatorial Guinea flag is a silk cotton tree. This tree, which is common in this region, is a national emblem of the country. Its seeds grow in pods surrounded by a fluffy fiber known as kapok. The silk cotton is one of the largest flowering trees in the world, reaching a height of 252 ft (77 m). The other countries with trees on their flags are Belize (mahogany tree), Bolivia (royal palm), Fiji (coconut palm), Haiti (royal palm), and Lebanon (cedar).

Kapok is used to stuff toys, mattresses, and pillows.

Angola's Machete and Gear

The emblem at the center of the flag of Angola is a half gear wheel, used in factory machinery, and a machete, a broad blade used by farmers for cutting crops. Together, these objects celebrate the country's workers. When the flag was designed for a newly independent Angola in 1975, the machete also remembered the armed struggle for independence from Portugal. The red, five-pointed star is an international symbol of socialism, a system of government in which workers, rather than companies, share ownership of factories and farms. The five points represent the five fingers of a worker's hand. Two other national flags feature farming tools: Belize (axes and a saw) and Mozambique (a hoe).

An Angolan farmer uses a machete to clear the ground of weeds, so she can plant coffee.

FLAG FOCUS: African Union

Type: International organization

In use: 2010–present

Flown by: The 55 member countries of the African Union, which works for peace and progress

Design: A silhouette of the African continent and its islands is positioned on a white sun, which symbolizes hope. The circle of 55 yellow, five-pointed stars represents the 55 member states. The number of stars has increased as new members join. The field is dark green, one of the Pan-African colors.

The star on Cameroon's flag stands for the unity of its people.

Fans support the Cameroon national football team, which has qualified for the FIFA World Cup more than any other African team.

THE INDOMITABLE LIONS
CAMEROON
PRIDE OF AFRICA

DID YOU KNOW? When the Cameroon flag was designed in 1957, many suggested it show a shrimp, after which the country is named (from the Portuguese "*camarões*").

Southern Africa

While most national flags have two, three, or four colors in their primary design, not including their central emblem, many southern African flags are more colorful. The South African flag is the joint record-holder, along with South Sudan, for having the most colors in its primary design: six. The flags in this region draw together their country's many different peoples and resources in a rainbow of color.

The African fish eagle, which appears on the flags of Zambia and Zimbabwe, is known for waking the region's people at dawn with its loud song.

SEYCHELLES

COMOROS

MALAWI

MOZAMBIQUE

ZAMBIA

ZIMBABWE

MADAGASCAR

NAMIBIA

BOTSWANA

MAURITIUS

ESWATINI

LESOTHO

SOUTH AFRICA

On the border between Zambia and Zimbabwe, the Victoria Falls ("Mosi-oa-Tunya" in Lozi) creates the world's largest sheet of falling water, with a width of 5,604 ft (1,708 m) and height of 354 ft (108 m).

ZAMBIA

A green field (representing plant life) is decorated with an African fish eagle, centered over stripes of red (freedom), black (the Zambian people), and orange (mineral wealth). The eagle represents the ability to rise above problems.

MALAWI

The current flag of Malawi was flown from 1964 to 2010, then readopted in 2012. It is a horizontal tricolor of black, red, and green, charged with a red rising sun. The sun represents the dawn of hope and freedom.

MOZAMBIQUE

On a red isosceles triangle, this flag bears a yellow five-pointed star, crossed with a hoe (for farming) and an AK-47 rifle (for defense), placed on an open book (signifying the importance of education).

COMOROS

The four stars and four stripes on the flag of Comoros represent the country's three main islands and a fourth island claimed by the nation. The crescent moon is a symbol of Islam (see page 30).

SEYCHELLES

The diagonal, ray-like bands in the flag of Seychelles symbolize progress and hope. The stripes are blue (sea and sky), yellow (sun and life), red (people and love), white (justice and peace), and green (land and plants).

MADAGASCAR

White and red were the colors of the Merina Kingdom, which ruled Madagascar until it was conquered by France in 1896. Green was the color of the Hova, the farmers who worked against French rule.

MAURITIUS

Adopted on independence in 1968, this flag has four horizontal stripes: red (for the struggle for freedom), blue (for the Indian Ocean), yellow (for the light of independence), and green (for farming).

NAMIBIA

In the flag of Namibia, blue represents the Atlantic Ocean, red stands for the Namibian people, green is for farming, and white is for peace. The yellow sun signifies life and energy.

BOTSWANA

The light blue field of the Botswana flag represents rain, which is especially precious in the region due to frequent droughts. The black and white stripes represent the zebra, the country's national animal.

ZIMBABWE

On a triangle at the hoist is a red star bearing a Zimbabwe Bird (see page 47). The flag's stripes stand for farming (green), mineral wealth (yellow), struggle (red), and the nation's people (black).

SOUTH AFRICA

The flag's black, gold, and green were taken from the flag of the African National Congress political party, which was led by Nelson Mandela, who was elected the country's first black president in 1994.

LESOTHO

Adopted in 2006, the flag of Lesotho bears a *mokorotlo* (see page 47). The blue stripe represents rain, the white stands for peace, and the green stripe symbolizes wealth and happiness.

ESWATINI

Representing a link with tradition, this flag bears a feathered staff, two spears, and a shield of the country's Nguni people. The black and white of the shield represent harmony between peoples.

DID YOU KNOW? The 31 rays of the sun on the flag of Malawi represent the fact that the country was the 31st African nation at the time of its independence.

The South African flag was first flown in 1994 during the country's first elections in which citizens of all races could take part.

The Y shape, known as a pall, is said to represent the coming together of all South Africa's peoples, who take the road ahead together.

DID YOU KNOW? The design of South Africa's flag was decided only seven days before it was first flown across the country, resulting in a scramble by the country's flag-makers.

Lesotho's Mokorotlo

Although several flags depict crowns or caps (see page 106) in their coat of arms, Lesotho's flag is the only one to be charged with just a hat. Known as a *mokorotlo*, this hat is the national symbol of Lesotho. Its shape is said to be inspired by the cone shape of Lesotho's Mt Qiloane. The *mokorotlo* protects the wearer from both sun and cold. The hat is also displayed in homes to show that the inhabitants respect tradition and hold close their bonds with their ancestors.

The *mokorotlo* is woven from a local grass called *mosea*.

The Zimbabwe Bird

Seventeen national flags feature birds, but only Zimbabwe's depicts a statue of a bird. The statue is in the style of eight soapstone sculptures found in the ruins of Great Zimbabwe. This city, surrounded by high walls, was built by ancestors of the Shona people in the 11th century. The statues were displayed on pillars in the city and on the walls. The birds are probably fish eagles, which may have been seen as messengers from the gods.

The Zimbabwe Bird sculptures have five-toed feet, like humans, instead of claws.

FLAG FOCUS: Mpumalanga

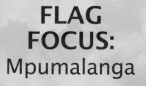

Type: Region

In use: 1996–present

Flown by: The province of Mpumalanga, in eastern South Africa

Design: In the upper left corner of the flag is a red Barberton daisy, which grows only in southeastern Africa. The zigzagging stripe of blue and white represents the region's Great Escarpment, a long cliff of rock, up to 11,424 ft (3,482 m) high, formed millions of years ago by the movement of plates of rock beneath Earth's surface.

East Asia

The national flags of East Asia look to the skies for inspiration. All these flags feature symbols of heavenly bodies: the sun, stars, or universe itself. The region's oldest flag is Japan's, which has been flying since 1870, although it was not adopted by law until 1999. The youngest is Mongolia's, which took its present form in 1992.

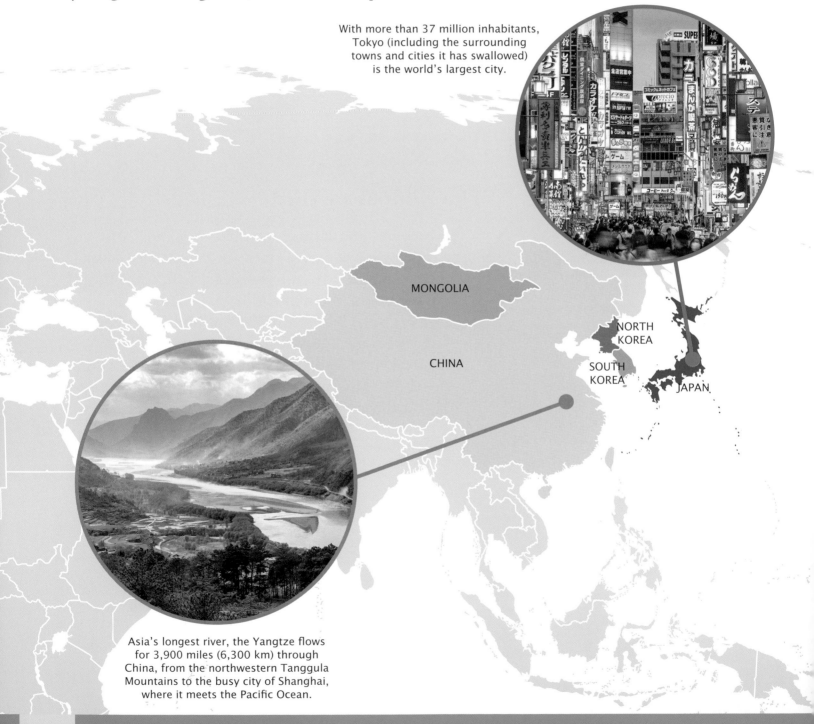

With more than 37 million inhabitants, Tokyo (including the surrounding towns and cities it has swallowed) is the world's largest city.

MONGOLIA

NORTH KOREA

CHINA

SOUTH KOREA

JAPAN

Asia's longest river, the Yangtze flows for 3,900 miles (6,300 km) through China, from the northwestern Tanggula Mountains to the busy city of Shanghai, where it meets the Pacific Ocean.

DID YOU KNOW? A North Korean flag weighing 600 lb (270 kg) flies on a 520 ft/160 m-tall flagpole over the North Korean village of Kijŏng-dong.

MONGOLIA

The flag of Mongolia took its current design in 1992. It is a triband of red, blue, and red, with a yellow *soyombo* symbol (see page 50) centered in the left-hand stripe. This symbol, representing unity and everlasting truths, was first depicted on the national flag in 1911. The blue stripe represents the sky, heaven, and eternity, while red symbolizes fire, progress, and happiness. The flag has a proportion of 1:2, which means that its width is twice its height.

CHINA

Adopted in 1949, the Chinese flag features five five-pointed golden stars in the upper left canton, on a red field. The largest star represents the Communist Party of China, the party that governs China. The four smaller stars represent China's people, who were once considered to be in four classes: workers, farmers, merchants, and business leaders. Traditionally, five is an important number in China, representing north, south, east, and west, plus China at the center.

NORTH KOREA

The flag of North Korea, first flown in 1948, has a broad horizontal red stripe (representing determination), bordered above and below by a narrow white stripe (symbolizing the unity of the nation's people) and a thicker blue stripe (standing for peace). To the left of the flag's center is a red, five-pointed star in a white circle. A red star is an international symbol of Communism, a system of government in which all property and businesses are shared.

SOUTH KOREA

Flown since 1948, this flag features a red and blue *taegeuk* (see page 50), with a trigram (a symbol made of three broken or unbroken bars) toward each of the four corners. Clockwise from top left, the trigrams are *geon* (symbolizing heaven), *gam* (the moon and water), *gon* (earth), and *ri* (the sun and fire). Together, they symbolize the harmony of all things. In Korean culture, the white field represents peace and purity.

JAPAN

The flag of Japan has a red circle, representing the sun (see page 50), centered on a white field. The flag's proportions are 2:3. By law, the correct size for the red circle is three-fifths of the flag's height. The sacred color of the gods, white represents purity and goodness. Red is the color of festivals, happiness, and prosperity. Traditionally, the color red was believed to frighten away evil spirits. Today, many Japanese temples and shrines are painted red. The emperor of Japan flies a red flag with a yellow chrysanthemum flower, a symbol of the imperial family, at is center.

The Sun

Japan's flag is one of 21 national flags that depict the sun. As our nearest star, the sun provides us with light and warmth, giving life to all Earth's living things. In all the flags on which it appears, the sun represents happiness, success, and progress. In Japan, the national flag is known as Nisshōki ("flag of the sun"). Japan's first sun flag was flown by Emperor Monmu, in the year 701. According to myth, Japanese emperors are descendants of the sun goddess Amaterasu. Today, Japan's emperor, Naruhito, attends ceremonies and welcomes visiting officials.

The sun goddess Amaterasu is one of the chief gods of Japan's Shinto religion.

The Universe

The flags of South Korea and Mongolia depict the universe. At the center of South Korea's flag is a red and blue *taegeuk*. This ancient symbol shows the universe's positive forces (red) and negative forces (blue), sometimes known as "yin and yang," which together create balance. A version of this symbol is seen on the left stripe of Mongolia's flag, where it forms part of a *soyombo*, the national symbol of Mongolia. The *soyombo* includes depictions of fire, the sun, the moon, two arrows (representing defeat of enemies), and four rectangles, providing stability and security. Both the *soyombo* and *taegeuk* express their nations' hopes for everlasting peace and happiness.

In Mongolia, the "yin and yang" symbol is often known as a *taijitu*.

Type: Region

In use: 1999–present

Flown by: The Special Administrative Region of Macau, in southern China

Design: At the center of the peacock green flag is a white lotus flower, the emblem of Macau. It rests on a simplified depiction of the 1974 Governor Nobre de Carvalho Bridge, which links mainland Macau with its island of Taipa, above white waves. The yellow stars are similar to the stars on the flag of China, of which Macau is a part.

Begun in the 7th century BCE, China's Great Wall eventually stretched over 13,000 miles (21,000 km).

The flag of China was adopted in 1949.

DID YOU KNOW? In modern China, red is the color of the ruling Communist Party, but the shade has been linked with happiness and good luck for many centuries.

South Asia

The South Asian flags use a variety of symbols, from a wheel to a dragon, to express their countries' history, beliefs, and hopes. The region is home to the only national flag that is not a rectangle or square: the flag of Nepal, a combination of two triangular pennants. In the past, the flags of most South Asian states were pennants, but only Nepal has kept the tradition.

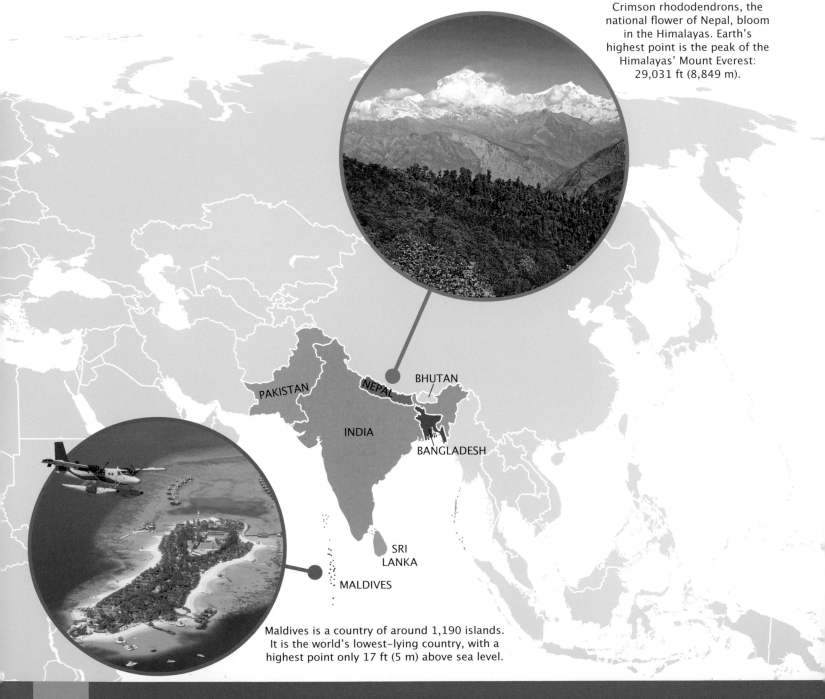

Crimson rhododendrons, the national flower of Nepal, bloom in the Himalayas. Earth's highest point is the peak of the Himalayas' Mount Everest: 29,031 ft (8,849 m).

PAKISTAN

NEPAL

BHUTAN

INDIA

BANGLADESH

SRI LANKA

MALDIVES

Maldives is a country of around 1,190 islands. It is the world's lowest-lying country, with a highest point only 17 ft (5 m) above sea level.

PAKISTAN

This flag's star and crescent moon (see page 30) is a symbol of Islam. In addition, the crescent moon represents progress, as a new moon grows over a month into a full moon, while the star symbolizes the light of education. The green background represents Islam: In the Quran, the Islamic holy book, green is the color of paradise. The white vertical stripe represents Pakistani citizens who follow other religions.

INDIA

The flag of India is a tricolor of saffron, white, and green. At the center of the white stripe is a 24-spoke wheel known as the wheel of dharma (see page 55). The saffron stripe stands for courage, the white for peace and truth, and the green for life and faith. For Hindus, Buddhists, and Sikhs, saffron—the color of the spice saffron—also represents the giving up of selfishness and material things.

NEPAL

The background of the flag of Nepal is crimson, the color of the national flower, the rhododendron. The blue border represents peace. The symbol in the upper triangle is a crescent moon, while the symbol in the lower triangle is a twelve-rayed sun. Together, the two emblems express the hope that Nepal will endure for as long as the sun and moon. Until 1962, these emblems both had human faces.

BHUTAN

This flag features a white thunder dragon, or *druk*. Most people in Bhutan follow the Drukpa ("Thunder Dragon") school of Buddhism. When the group's founder, Tsangpa Gyare, set up his first monastery in 1180, he heard thunder, said to be the voice of a dragon. Bhutan is known to its people as Druk Yul ("Land of the Thunder Dragon"). The dragon holds jewels to represent wealth. The current design was adopted in 1969.

BANGLADESH

The flag of Bangladesh is one of three national flags (along with Japan and Palau) to feature only a circle. The circle is positioned slightly to the left of the flag's center so it appears to be centered when the flag is flying. The red stands for the people of Bangladesh, while the green represents their land. The flag was adopted in 1972, after Bangladesh gained independence from Pakistan. The flag has a proportion of 3:5.

MALDIVES

Adopted in 1965, this flag has a white crescent moon on a green rectangle, centered on a red field. The green of the rectangle and the crescent moon (see page 30) are both symbols of Islam, the religion of the majority of the country's people. The red border is a reminder of the plain red flag that was flown by the islands until the early 20th century, when it was decided that Maldives needed a more distinctive design.

SRI LANKA

This flag has two panels, bordered by yellow. The left panel has stripes of green (for the country's Muslims) and saffron (for its Tamil people). The larger, maroon panel features a lion, a symbol of the country's Sinhalese people (see page 55), which holds a sword to signify strength. In each corner of this panel is a bo leaf, representing the four Buddhist virtues of kindness, compassion, joy, and calm.

DID YOU KNOW? The Pakistan flag is mentioned in the third verse of the national anthem: "The flag of the crescent and star, Leads the way to progress and perfection ..."

53

In Bhutan, a monk wears a dragon mask to perform a traditional dance.

As on the national flag, the dragon bares its teeth to protect Buddhism and its people.

FLAG FOCUS: Punjab, Pakistan

Type: Region

In use: 1970–present

Flown by: The province of Punjab, in eastern Pakistan

Design: The flag uses the Pakistani national colors of white and dark green, as well as the star and crescent pictured on the national flag. In the central circle are five wavy lines, representing the five rivers that give the province its name, from the Persian *panj* (five) and *ab* (waters). The circle rests on ears of wheat, one of the province's main crops. The inscription reads "Government of Punjab" in the Shahmukhi alphabet.

DID YOU KNOW? The largest ever human national flag was made in 2014 by 43,830 people holding colored cards to create the Indian flag.

Gandhi's Wheel

Gandhi encouraged peaceful protest, such as spinning thread on a wheel, to gain independence from Britain.

India's peaceful fight for independence from Britain was led by Mohandas Gandhi (1869–1948). He did not want Indians to rely on buying cloth from Britain, so he encouraged people to make their own thread using a spinning wheel. In 1921, during the campaign for independence, Gandhi suggested a new flag for India with a spinning wheel at its center. In 1947, when India finally achieved independence, the spinning wheel was swapped for the wheel of dharma ("law"). This symbol is used in the Indian religions of Hinduism, Jainism, and Buddhism. It represents everlasting truths as well as progress.

Sri Lanka's Lion

The lion on Sri Lanka's flag represents its Sinhalese people, who make up around three-quarters of the population. Sinhalese means "of lions" in the ancient South Asian language Sanskrit. According to legend, the first Sinhalese king of Sri Lanka was Vijaya, who arrived on the island in 543 BCE, with hundreds of supporters, from an Indian city known as Sinhapura ("Lion City"). King Vijaya was said to be descended from a lion and had a lion's strength. Many later Sri Lankan rulers used lions as a symbol of their power. The Asiatic lion was common in India until the late 19th century, but it was never found in Sri Lanka.

In Sri Lanka's capital, Colombo, lion statues guard a monument celebrating independence from British rule, in 1948.

Southeast Asia

Red appears on all the flags of Southeast Asia, yet each country gives the color a slightly different meaning. For Thailand, red represents the land and its people. For Vietnam, red is the blood shed during struggles for independence. For Malaysia, red represents bravery and strength. In Cambodia, red is a color of happiness and wisdom for the nation's Buddhists.

On the island of Luzon in the Philippines, rice is grown on flat terraces carved from the hillsides. The country's three main island groups—Luzon, Mindanao, and the Visayas—are represented by three stars on the national flag.

MYANMAR

LAOS

THAILAND

CAMBODIA VIETNAM

PHILIPPINES

BRUNEI

MALAYSIA

SINGAPORE

INDONESIA

EAST TIMOR

In Laos, a golden statue of the Buddha overlooks the Mekong River. Vital for water, transport, and trade, the 3,050 mile/ 4,909 km–long Mekong is represented on the country's flag.

DID YOU KNOW? When the Philippines is at war, the national flag is flown upside down, with the red stripe at the top.

MYANMAR

Adopted in 2010, Myanmar's tricolor represents unity (yellow), peace (green), and courage (red). The white five-pointed star signifies the union of the country's peoples, which include Burman, Karen, Shan, Kachin, and Chin.

LAOS

The blue stripe represents Laos's major river, the Mekong, while the white circle signifies both unity and the moon reflected in the river. The red stripes stand for the struggle for independence from France.

VIETNAM

Vietnam's flag features a large yellow star on a red field. The star's five points represent the five traditional classes of people: workers, farmers, soldiers, intellectuals (for example, teachers), and business leaders.

THAILAND

First flown in 1917, the Thai flag has stripes of red (for the people), white (for religion), and blue (for the royal family). The flag flown by Thailand's navy has the addition of a white elephant at its center.

CAMBODIA

With an unusual proportion of 16:25, the flag of Cambodia took its current design in 1993. At the flag's center is a depiction of the temple of Angkor (see page 58). The blue stripes stand for freedom and co-operation.

PHILIPPINES

The Philippines' blue stripe stands for peace and truth, while the red represents courage. On a white triangle is an eight-rayed sun, symbolizing the first eight provinces. The current design was adopted in 1998.

MALAYSIA

The 14 red and white stripes and 14-pointed star signify the country's 14 states and territories. The crescent moon is a symbol of Islam (see page 30). The yellow of the moon and star is the traditional color of Malay rulers.

BRUNEI

The colors of Brunei's flag represent the government: the sultan (yellow) and his advisers (black and white). At the center is Brunei's crest (see page 58), which uses upturned hands to show the government's care of its people.

INDONESIA

First flown in 1945, the flag of Indonesia looks almost identical to the flag of Monaco, but it is wider and its red stripe is brighter. Traditionally, its colors represent earth (red) and sky (white).

SINGAPORE

For Singapore, red represents equality and white is for purity. The crescent (growing) moon stands for progress, while the five stars stand for five ideals: peace, democracy, progress, justice, and equality.

EAST TIMOR

This flag has two overlapping triangles at the hoist, in black (representing the period when East Timor was ruled by foreign powers) and yellow (the struggle for independence). The white star signifies hope for the future.

Angkor Wat

Since 1863, the Cambodian flag has featured Angkor Wat, one of the world's largest temples. When it was first built, in the 12th century, Angkor Wat was a Hindu temple, but it became a Buddhist temple later that century. The temple has five towers, although not all can be seen on the flag. These towers represent the five peaks of the mythical Meru, a holy mountain for both Hindus and Buddhists. Meru, which reaches into the heavens, is the home of the gods. On the Cambodian flag, the temple represents both the country's religious beliefs and its long history.

Angkor Wat is surrounded by moats, which represent the seven seas that surround Meru.

The Sultan's Parasol

The flag of Brunei expresses respect for its ruler, the sultan. The sultan is one of the world's few absolute monarchs, which means he holds supreme power. Yellow (seen in the flag's field) is the traditional color of royalty. At the top of the flag's red crest is a swallowtail flag and a parasol, called a *payung ubor-ubor*, which are both used by the Sultan. The sultan sits under a *payung ubor-ubor*, covered in yellow silk, during ceremonies. The parasol's outstretched wings represent the protection the sultan should offer to the country's people.

Sultan Hassanal Bolkiah has ruled Brunei since 1967.

Indonesia's national youth group Paskibraka has responsibility for raising the flag on Independence Day.

FLAG FOCUS:
Association of Southeast Asian Nations

Type: International organization

In use: 1997–present

Flown by: The 10 countries that are members of the Association of Southeast Asian Nations, which works for wealth and progress in the region

Design: The colors of the flag—blue, red, yellow, and white—are the main colors of the flags of its member countries. In addition, blue represents peace, red is for progress, white stands for honesty, and yellow is for wealth. The 10 countries are represented by 10 stalks of rice, one of the region's major crops.

The flag must be extended before it is raised.

DID YOU KNOW? The Vietnam flag is the only Southeast Asian flag that does not include white, as red and yellow have been the national colors for centuries.

West Asia

In this region, many countries use colors, symbols, or inscriptions (writing) to symbolize the religion followed by the majority of their people. In Israel, that religion is Judaism, while in much of the region, it is Islam. Many Arabic-speaking countries use the Pan-Arab colors of black, white, green, and red. In the 14th century, these colors were described by the Arab poet Safi al-Din al-Hilli: "White are our deeds, black are our battles, Green are our fields, red are our swords."

The world's tallest building, the United Arab Emirates' Burj Khalifa reaches a height of 2,722 ft (829.8 m).

TURKEY

CYPRUS
LEBANON
PALESTINE
ISRAEL

SYRIA

IRAQ

IRAN

JORDAN

KUWAIT
BAHRAIN
QATAR

SAUDI
ARABIA

UNITED
ARAB
EMIRATES

OMAN

YEMEN

The world's largest mosque is the Masjid al-Haram, in Mecca, the birthplace of the Prophet Muhammad and a place of pilgrimage for all Muslims.

TURKEY

This flag was the first to feature a star and crescent, today an international symbol of Islam (see page 30). The flag's proportion (2:3) and exact shade of red were standardized in 1936.

CYPRUS

The Cypriot flag features the island's outline in copper, with two olive branches to signify peace between the country's Greek and Turkish communities. The white field also symbolizes peace.

SYRIA

At the time of writing, there are two main Syrian flags, one flown by the government (above) and one by the key opposition, with a green rather than red stripe, plus three red stars instead of two green.

IRAQ

Iraq adopted its current flag in 2008. The tricolor is charged with an Arabic phrase known as the Takbir: "Allāhu ʾakbar," meaning "God is the greatest." The flag has a proportion of 2:3.

IRAN

This tricolor has the Takbir written in white 22 times across the green and red stripes. The central emblem is a stylized representation of the word "Allah," or "God," composed of a sword and crescents.

LEBANON

The flag of Lebanon is a Spanish fess (a triband in which the central stripe is twice the height of the other two stripes). A green cedar (see page 62) touches both of the red stripes.

ISRAEL

This flag has been flown by Israel since 1948. At its center is the Star of David, a symbol of Judaism. The design reflects the white and blue- or black-striped *tallit*, a shawl worn during prayer.

PALESTINE

The Palestine flag displays the Pan-Arab colors in three equal stripes, plus a chevron (a triangle at the hoist). It was first flown by the Palestinian Liberation Organization in 1964.

JORDAN

Like the flag of Palestine, Jordan's flag features a red chevron. Within the chevron is a white seven-pointed star, representing Al-Fatiha: the seven verses of the first chapter of the Quran.

KUWAIT

The flag of Kuwait is a tricolor with a black trapezium (a four-sided shape with at least one pair of parallel sides) at the hoist. First flown in 1961, the flag has a proportion of 1:2.

SAUDI ARABIA

Flown since 1973, this flag has a green field, symbolizing Islam. The inscription reads: "There is no god but Allah; Muhammad is the Messenger of Allah." The sword signifies strictness in applying justice.

BAHRAIN

With a proportion of 3:5, the flag of Bahrain has a white band with five triangles, signifying the Five Pillars of Islam, which are the acts that all Muslims must perform, including prayer and charity.

QATAR

Qatar's flag is similar to Bahrain's, but is maroon and has nine white triangles, representing Qatar's historical position as one of nine regional Arab emirates. With a proportion of 11:28, it is the only national flag with a width more than twice its height.

UNITED ARAB EMIRATES

Flown since 1971, the flag of the United Arab Emirates features the Pan-Arab colors. For Emiratis, these colors also signify courage (red), love and hope (green), honesty and peace (white), and strength of mind (black).

OMAN

The flag of Oman features the national emblem (see page 62) in its upper left corner. The current flag design (with a wider horizontal red stripe than the previous design) was adopted in 1995. Its proportions are 1:2.

YEMEN

Adopted in 1990, the flag of Yemen uses the colors of the Arab Liberation flag (first flown during the Egyptian Revolution of 1952). The flag of the president has the addition of an eagle in its top left corner.

DID YOU KNOW? The largest flag ever flown was a United Arab Emirates flag of 26,356 sq ft (2,448.56 sq m) in 2017.

The Cedars of Lebanon

The tree at the center of the Lebanon flag is the cedar of Lebanon. Found only in the mountains of Lebanon, Turkey, Syria, and Cyprus, this tree's needle-shaped leaves stay on the branches throughout the snowy winter. The cedar is mentioned 77 times in the Bible, which was written down in this region over more than a thousand years, starting from around 1200 BCE. In the Bible's Book of Psalms, a good person is likened to a strong, tall cedar: "The righteous shall flourish like the palm tree: He shall grow like a cedar in Lebanon." The tree is the national emblem of Lebanon, a symbol of the country's strength and growth.

The cedar of Lebanon grows up to 130 ft (40 m) tall.

The Khanjar of Oman

In the top left corner of the Omani flag is the national emblem: two crossed swords and a curved dagger known as a *khanjar*, inside its sheath. The weapons are linked by a decorated waist belt. The emblem was used by the Omani royal family from the 18th century, but did not appear on the national flag until 1970. Although *khanjars* were once used as weapons and for hunting, today's Omani men wear them for ceremonies, weddings, and parades. The *khanjar* represents Oman's history as well as its strength.

A *khanjar* is often given as a gift to a groom when he gets married.

Turkish students parade on October 29, celebrating the day in 1923 that the last sultan stepped down and Turkey became a republic.

DID YOU KNOW? Asia's oldest national flag is Turkey's, which was adopted in 1844, when Turkey was part of the Ottoman Empire.

Osman I, the first sultan of the Ottoman Empire in 1299, is said to have seen a crescent moon in a dream.

FLAG FOCUS:
Amman

Type: City

In use: 2009–present

Flown by: Amman, the capital of Jordan

Design: Across the foreground, the word "Amman" is written in Arabic in a simplified script. Blending with the word, and also in yellow, is a building with arches in the regional style, suggesting the city's mosques and palaces. In the background, three brown crescents represent the city's 19 hills.

The Caucasus and Central Asia

The flags of this region celebrate the religions, traditions, stories, and crafts of their peoples. Both the Kazakhstan and Turkmenistan flags represent local crafts in a vertical stripe near the hoist edge. With its seven stars, the flag of Tajikistan remembers traditional stories, where the number seven has great importance, from seven heavenly mountains to seven tests of the hero's strength.

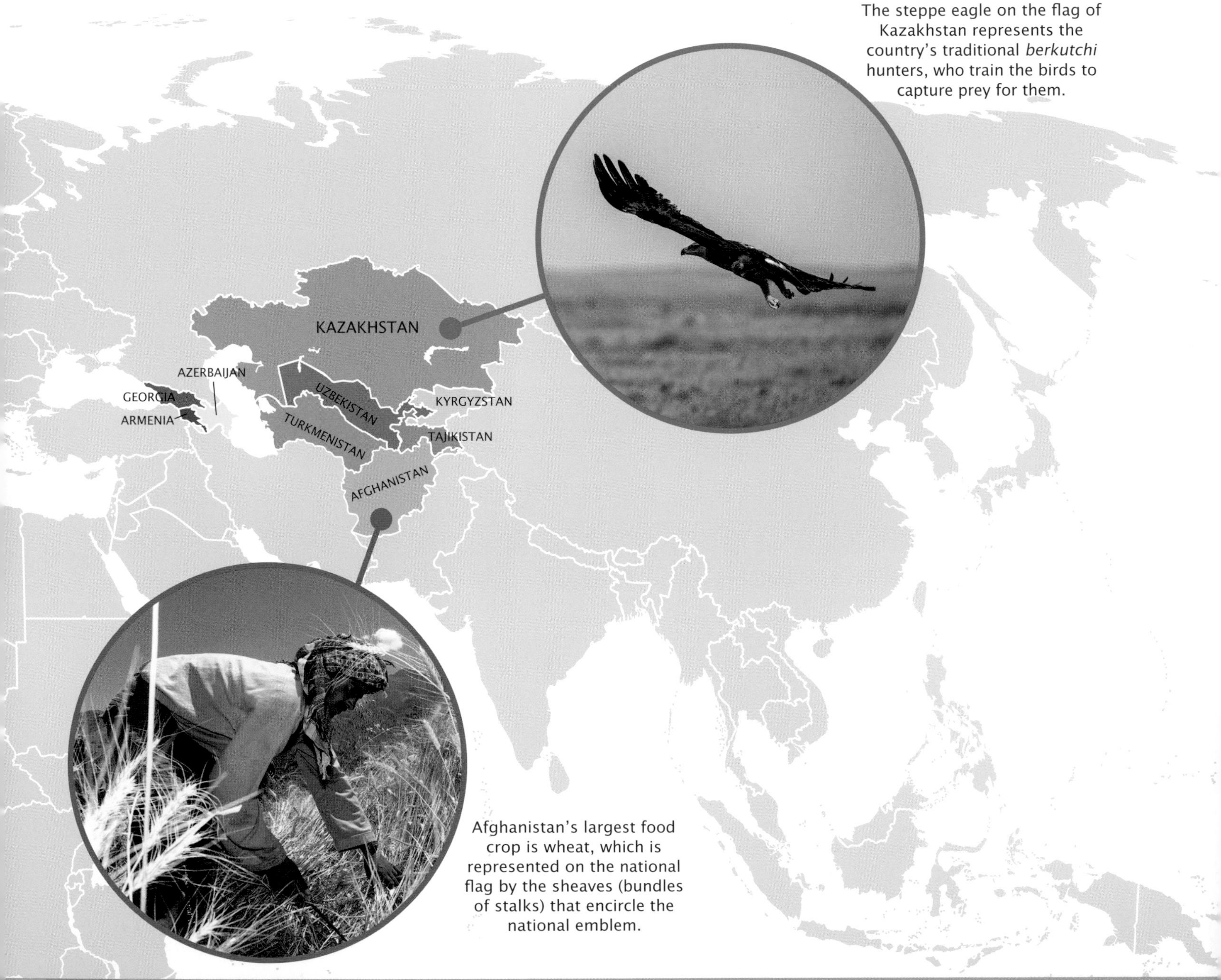

The steppe eagle on the flag of Kazakhstan represents the country's traditional *berkutchi* hunters, who train the birds to capture prey for them.

KAZAKHSTAN

AZERBAIJAN

GEORGIA

ARMENIA

UZBEKISTAN

KYRGYZSTAN

TURKMENISTAN

TAJIKISTAN

AFGHANISTAN

Afghanistan's largest food crop is wheat, which is represented on the national flag by the sheaves (bundles of stalks) that encircle the national emblem.

GEORGIA

The flag of Georgia was adopted in 2004, although a similar flag was flown by the Kingdom of Georgia from around 1008 to 1490. The flag features a large central red cross, with a Bolnisi cross in each quarter. These crosses have arms that are narrower at the center than the edges, a design taken from a 5th-century cross at the Bolnisi Sioni cathedral in southern Georgia and today a symbol of the nation.

ARMENIA

Adopted in 1990, the Armenian flag is a tricolor of red, blue, and orange. Red represents Christianity, the Armenian people's past struggle for survival, and freedom. Blue stands for the desire to live beneath peaceful skies, while orange signifies the nation's creativity and hard work. The flag is mentioned in the national anthem: "Look at it, the three colors/ Which are our gifted symbol."

AZERBAIJAN

Azerbaijan's flag was flown between 1918 and 1920, then readopted in 1991. The green stripe, as well as the central crescent moon and eight-pointed star (see page 30), are symbols of Islam. The light blue is a color used to represent Turkic peoples, who live across western, central, and northeastern Asia. The red stripe symbolizes progress and democracy.

KAZAKHSTAN

Like the flag of Azerbaijan, the Kazakhstan flag uses light blue to represent its Turkic peoples, in addition to the wide skies over its grasslands (known as steppe). The soaring steppe eagle represents freedom, while the sun, its rays shaped like grain, stands for prosperity. Near the hoist is a *koshkar-muiz* ("horns of the ram") pattern, which is often used in traditional crafts.

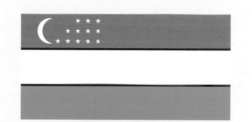

UZBEKISTAN

The blue stripe of this tricolor represents Turkic peoples. White stands for peace and kindness. Green represents Islam and nature. The red fimbriations signify the life of all the country's peoples, animals, and plants. The crescent moon and 12 stars represent Islam (see page 30), with the stars arranged so that when joined together by two lines they spell out the word Allah in Arabic.

KYRGYZSTAN

The flag of Kyrgyzstan has a red field with a yellow sun containing a *tunduk* (see page 67) at its center. The sun has 40 rays, representing the word "Kyrgyz," which may come from the Turkic word for 40, a reference to the people's 40 tribes. The red field is inspired by the legendary hero Manas, who flew a red battle flag and whose adventures are described in the famous poem *Epic of Manas*.

TURKMENISTAN

Turkmenistan's flag took its current design in 2001, after changes to its proportions. In a stripe near the hoist are five carpet guls (see page 66) above olive branches, representing peace. The green field, as well as the crescent moon and stars, represent Islam. In addition, the five stars symbolize the five senses, and their five points represent states of matter: solid, crystal, gas, liquid, and plasma.

TAJIKISTAN

In this tricolor, the white stripe is one and a half times the height of the others. The white represents purity, the snow of the mountains, and the important crop of cotton. The red stripe signifies victory and sunrise. The green stripe stands for Islam, fields, and forests. The central crown represents the Tajik people, as many believe the word Tajik comes from the Persian word for crown: *tâj*.

AFGHANISTAN

In the Afghan flag, which is in dispute at the time of writing, the black stripe represents the country's often troubled history, red stands for progress, and green symbolizes Islam. At the center is the national emblem, containing a mosque flying two Afghan flags. On a ribbon is the year 1298 in the Afghan calendar, equal to the year 1919, when the country gained independence.

DID YOU KNOW? The flag of Georgia features the most crosses of any national flag, five, followed by the flag of Fiji, with four.

Carpet Weaving

Turkmenistan is famous for its carpets, which have been woven by Turkmen women for hundreds of years. Traditionally, the carpets were woven in wool that had been colored by vegetable dyes. In a red stripe on the flag of Turkmenistan are five carpet guls, which are patterns that often form an octagon. A gul is usually symmetrical and contains shapes or flowers. Traditionally, different tribes weave different guls. The five shown on the flag represent five of the country's tribes: Teke, Yomut, Arsary, Chowdur, and Saryk.

A Turkmen weaver draws through a horizontal "weft" thread, moving it over and under the "warp" threads, which are held in place by a loom.

This national flag measures 98 ft by 197 ft (30 m by 60 m).

At 541 ft (165 m), the flagpole at Dushanbe, in Tajikistan, is the world's second tallest.

FLAG FOCUS:
Nur–Sultan

Type: City

In use: 2019–present

Flown by: Nur–Sultan, the capital of Kazakhstan

Design: With its turquoise and gold color scheme, the flag matches the national flag. The sun's rays stretching from the central circle reflect the city's name, which means "Lord of Light" in Kazakh. Inside the circle are a depiction of the crossed beams at the top of a yurt, as seen in the flag of Turkmenistan, and a simplified drawing of the city's Baiterek Tower.

Waking in a Yurt

A yurt is a circular tent that was lived in by the peoples of Central Asia as they moved with their horses, sheep, cows, or goats to find fresh water and grass. Today, few Central Asian people still live in yurts. The peoples of Kyrgyzstan used a yurt made of wooden poles, covered with felt cloth, made from matted animal hair. At the top of a Kyrgyz yurt is an opening called a *tunduk*, crisscrossed by poles. A *tunduk* is shown at the center of the Kyrgyzstan flag, inside a sun. This represents the first sight of someone waking in a yurt in the morning. The emblem symbolizes life, home, and history.

A Kyrgyz yurt is often constructed from willow poles, which are bent while being steamed.

DID YOU KNOW? The flag of Uzbekistan has the third highest number of stars of any national flag, 12, behind Brazil with 27 and the United States with 50.

Ireland and the United Kingdom

Lying on two large islands and 6,000 smaller ones are the countries of the Republic of Ireland and the United Kingdom. The United Kingdom is itself made up of four countries: England, Northern Ireland, Scotland, and Wales. The flag of the United Kingdom is the Union Flag, or Union Jack. England, Scotland, and Wales also have their own flag, while Northern Ireland flies several flags to represent its communities.

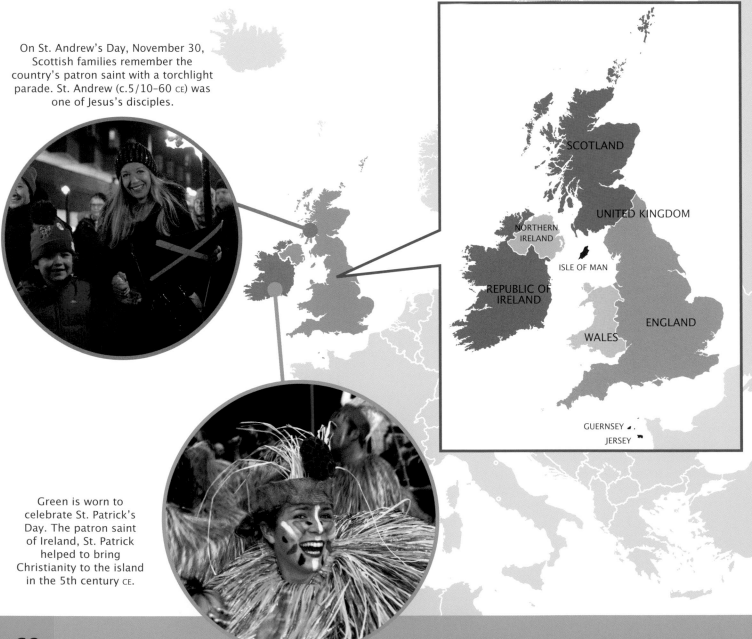

On St. Andrew's Day, November 30, Scottish families remember the country's patron saint with a torchlight parade. St. Andrew (c.5/10–60 CE) was one of Jesus's disciples.

SCOTLAND

UNITED KINGDOM

NORTHERN IRELAND

ISLE OF MAN

REPUBLIC OF IRELAND

ENGLAND

WALES

GUERNSEY

JERSEY

Green is worn to celebrate St. Patrick's Day. The patron saint of Ireland, St. Patrick helped to bring Christianity to the island in the 5th century CE.

REPUBLIC OF IRELAND

The Republic of Ireland's flag was first flown in 1848, 74 years before it was adopted as the national flag when Ireland gained independence from the United Kingdom. The tricolor design was inspired by the French flag (see page 77). The green was intended to symbolize the country's Roman Catholics, while the orange represented its Protestants. The white band stood for the peace between these two branches of Christianity. Today, the flag represents the unity of all the country's different peoples and traditions.

UNITED KINGDOM

The Union Jack is a combination of three flags, each composed of a cross. In 1606, the flags of England (see below right) and Scotland (see below left) were joined for the first time. Northern Ireland is represented by St. Patrick's Saltire, a diagonal red cross on a white field. It was added to the Union Flag in 1800. Wales is the only country of the United Kingdom not represented on the flag, because Wales and England were legally joined from 1535, before national flags were commonly flown.

Three of the Constituent Countries of the United Kingdom

SCOTLAND

The St. Andrew's Saltire is a white diagonal cross on a blue field. Its design comes from the belief that St. Andrew was crucified on a diagonal cross. The symbol was flown and worn by Scottish armies from medieval times. By the early 16th century, the saltire was flown on ships of the Scottish navy.

WALES

Y Ddraig Goch ("The Red Dragon"), has been flown since at least 1485, but adopted its current design in 1959. The flag features the red dragon of Wales (see page 70) on green and white stripes, the colors of the House of Tudor, the Welsh family that held the English throne from 1485 to 1603.

ENGLAND

The St. George's Cross, a symmetrical red cross on a white background, was flown or worn by English soldiers from around 1270. The symbol was linked with St. George, a Roman soldier who was killed for his Christian faith. He was designated England's main patron saint in the middle of the 16th century.

Crown Dependencies of the United Kingdom

The three Crown Dependencies are self-governing territories that lie off the coast of the United Kingdom. The government of the United Kingdom is responsible for their defense.

ISLE OF MAN

The flag of the Isle of Man, adopted in 1932, is based on the island's 13th-century coat of arms. It features three armored legs, similar to those seen on the flag of Sicily (see page 83), possibly due to family links between the medieval rulers of the two islands.

GUERNSEY

Before 1985, when a flag was designed to avoid confusion in sporting events, Guernsey flew the English flag. The flag has a St. George's Cross with a gold cross representing the Normans, who ruled northern France in the Middle Ages and from whom many islanders are descended.

JERSEY

Adopted in 1981, the flag of Jersey takes precedence over the flag of the United Kingdom, which means it may be flown higher or to its left. A red saltire has represented Jersey since at least the 18th century. Above the cross is Jersey's coat of arms, featuring three gold leopards.

DID YOU KNOW? When the Republic of Ireland's flag is flown, it should be taken down if it becomes frayed, touches the ground or water, or becomes tangled in trees.

The Dragon of Wales

The flags of Wales, Bhutan (see page 53), and Malta (see page 81) feature dragons. These legendary scaly creatures appear in stories across the world. In Asia, dragons are usually wingless. In Europe, dragons are winged and able to breathe fire. Around the year 830, the Welsh story about its red dragon was first written down, but it was probably based on stories told for years. The story describes a battle between a red dragon and a white dragon. The red dragon represents the Britons while the white dragon represents the Saxons. The Britons had lived in Britain for hundreds of years before the Saxons started to arrive from mainland Europe in the 5th century. The Britons were pushed into western regions such as Wales. Today's Welsh language developed from the language spoken by the Britons.

The Union Flag flies over the Victoria Tower of the UK's Houses of Parliament.

This 15th–century illustration shows the long battle between the white dragon and red dragon, which was finally victorious.

DID YOU KNOW? The Union Flag may be called the Union Jack because it was flown on British navy ships as a small flag at the bow (front), known as a "jack."

FLAG FOCUS: Coventry

Type: City

In use: 2018–present

Flown by: Coventry, in the West Midlands region of England

Design: At the center of the flag is Lady Godiva, the wife of Leofric, Earl of Mercia, who ruled the city in the 11th century. According to legend, Godiva rode through the city naked, covered only by her long hair, to protest against the high taxes that her husband was demanding from Coventry.

The flag of Ireland's president, known as the Presidential Standard, is flown on their official car.

When the Queen enters the Houses of Parliament, the Union Flag is swapped for her flag, the Royal Standard.

The Harp of Ireland

The emblem of the Republic of Ireland is a harp, which appears on the flag of Ireland's president, its navy, and its capital city, Dublin. The harp is also on Irish passports and coins. The harp shown on these flags and objects is based on a harp on display in Trinity College Dublin, once said to belong to the 10th-century Irish king Brian Boru but actually dating from the 15th century. In medieval Ireland, harps were played in the courts of Ireland's many kings. After England's Henry VIII became King of Ireland in 1542, those courts and their harpists fell silent. In defiance of English kings, the harp became a symbol of Irish culture.

North Europe

All the Nordic (from the regional words for "north") countries—Iceland, Norway, Sweden, Finland, and Denmark—have a Nordic cross on their flag. A Nordic cross has the center of the cross shifted toward the hoist side of the flag. Estonia, Latvia, and Lithuania are known as the Baltic states because they lie on the eastern shore of the Baltic Sea. They all have flags with three horizontal bands.

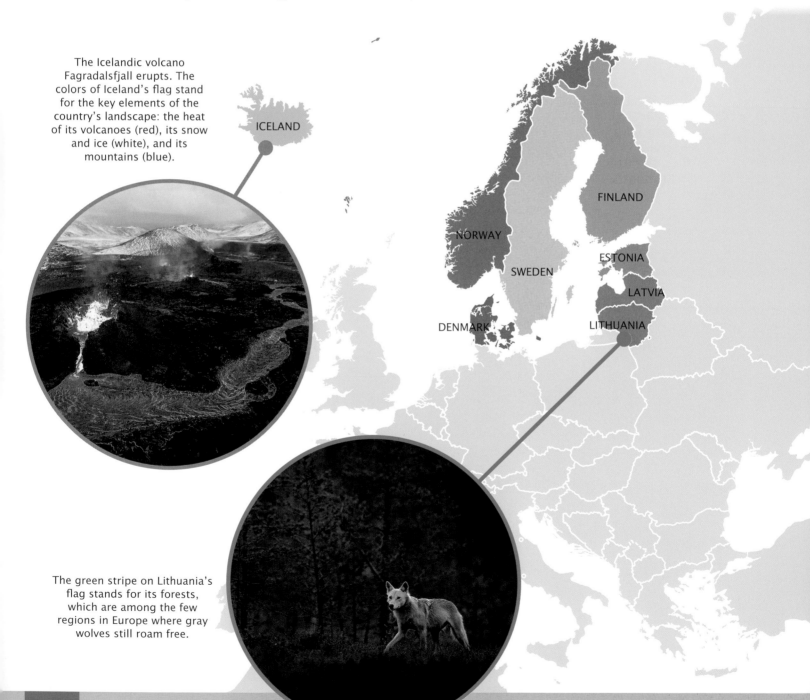

The Icelandic volcano Fagradalsfjall erupts. The colors of Iceland's flag stand for the key elements of the country's landscape: the heat of its volcanoes (red), its snow and ice (white), and its mountains (blue).

ICELAND

FINLAND

NORWAY

ESTONIA

SWEDEN

LATVIA

DENMARK

LITHUANIA

The green stripe on Lithuania's flag stands for its forests, which are among the few regions in Europe where gray wolves still roam free.

ICELAND

The Icelandic flag is a white-edged red Nordic cross on a blue field. The flag's proportions are 18:25. Like the flags of the other Nordic countries, Iceland's flag is based on the flag of Denmark, which had dominance over the island from 1380 to 1918. The current colors and proportions, closely based on an earlier design by historian Matthías Þórðarson, date from 1944, when Iceland became a republic.

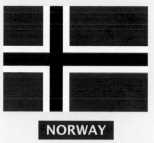

NORWAY

With a proportion of 8:11, the flag of Norway has a white-edged dark blue Nordic cross on a red field. The flag was first adopted in 1821. It was based on the Danish flag, which had been flown by Norway while the two countries were part of a union. A blue cross was added to the Norwegian flag to make it distinctive. Red, white, and blue, as used in the French tricolor, were seen as symbolic of freedom.

SWEDEN

A yellow Nordic cross on a blue field, the current design of the Swedish flag was adopted in 1906. Yellow and blue may have started to be used as the national colors when they appeared in the coat of arms of King Magnus III in 1275. The Nordic cross was inspired by the flag of Denmark, with which Sweden had periods of both rivalry and union. The flag's proportions are 5:8.

FINLAND

The *Siniristilippu* ("Blue Cross Flag") was adopted in 1918, after Finland gained independence from Russia. The blue represents the country's 180,000 lakes, while the white symbolizes the winter snow. The flag was designed by artists Eero Snellman and Bruno Tuukkanen, inspired by the flags of the other Nordic countries. The flag has a proportion of 11:18, making it the widest of the Nordic flags.

DENMARK

The Danish flag is a white Nordic cross on a red field, with a proportion somewhere between 28:34 and 28:37. Used by Danish armies since possibly as early as 1219 (see page 74), the flag became popular among Danish citizens in the 19th century as a symbol of their nation. The royal standard of Denmark has the addition of the monarch's coat of arms in a white square.

ESTONIA

This flag was flown by Estonia from 1922 to 1940, then readopted in 1990. In his famous song "Eesti Lipp" ("The Estonian Flag"), the Estonian poet Martin Lipp linked the tricolor's blue with the sky, black with Estonia's soil, and white with purity and hard work. The naval ensign is a swallowtail (see page 74) with the addition of the national coat of arms.

LATVIA

The flag of Latvia has a white stripe (one fifth the height of the flag) on a carmine (dark red) field. Legend tells us the design was born in the Middle Ages, when a Latvian tribal leader was killed in battle and wrapped in a white sheet that was soon stained by his blood. Today, the flag's color symbolizes Latvians' willingness to defend their nation's liberty.

LITHUANIA

This flag was flown between 1918 and 1940, then readopted in 1989 (although its proportion was changed from 1:2 to 3:5 in 2004). The triband's colors were chosen because they were often used in traditional Lithuanian dress and handicrafts. In addition, yellow stands for the sun and prosperity, green for forests and freedom, and red for bravery.

DID YOU KNOW? One of the world's oldest flags, the Latvian flag was first flown by battling Latvian tribes in 1280, but it was not adopted as the national flag until 1918.

The Dannebrog

The Danish flag, known as the Dannebrog, is probably the world's oldest continuously used national flag. We know the flag was flown by the kings of Denmark from the 14th century. A legend tells that it was first flown even earlier, in 1219. The story goes that the flag magically fell from the sky during the Battle of Lyndanisse, giving the Danish soldiers the strength they needed to defeat their enemies. Like the flag of many Christian countries, the Dannebrog was a cross, a representation of the cross on which Christ was crucified. The Dannebrog was a centered cross until 1748, when it was ruled that Danish ships should move the vertical portion of the cross toward the hoist to make the left quarters into neat squares.

The falling of a flag marked with a cross is said to have brought victory to the Danish King Valdemar II (seated) in 1219.

The Swedish army flies the country's triple-tailed flag.

Swallowtails

The Nordic countries share not only the Nordic cross but the use of a swallowtail flag, which has a V-shaped cut creating two points, or tails, at the fly. Sometimes, the swallowtail has a third tail, known as a tongue, between the two other tails. The swallowtail is used as a variant, or alternative, flag flown for official purposes rather than by ordinary citizens and businesses. It can be flown by the government, navy, or army.

The Norwegian swallowtail flag flies over the country's parliament building, the Stortinget.

DID YOU KNOW? The Scottish islands of Barra, Orkney, Shetland, and South Uist have Nordic cross flags, reflecting the fact they were once ruled by Norway.

The Royal Guards at Stockholm Palace perform the ceremony of the changing of the guard, when fresh guards take over duty.

FLAG FOCUS: Sámi

Type: Cultural or ethnic group

In use: 1986–present

Flown by: Sámi people, the Sámi region, and, on National Sámi Day, all government buildings in Norway

Design: The colors of the flag are popular on the traditional *gákti* tunic worn by Sámi, the indigenous people of northern Norway, Sweden, Finland, and Russia. The circle represents both the sun (red) and moon (blue), because the Sámi national anthem, as well as many legends, call the Sámi the children of the sun.

West Europe

Many of the flags in this region have a long history. The oldest of these flags in continuous use—and also the world's first national tricolor—is the Netherlands', which has flown since 1660. It inspired both the Russian and French flags, which themselves inspired many others. The youngest flag in West Europe is Spain's, adopted in 1981, although it is very similar to a flag flown by the Spanish navy from 1785.

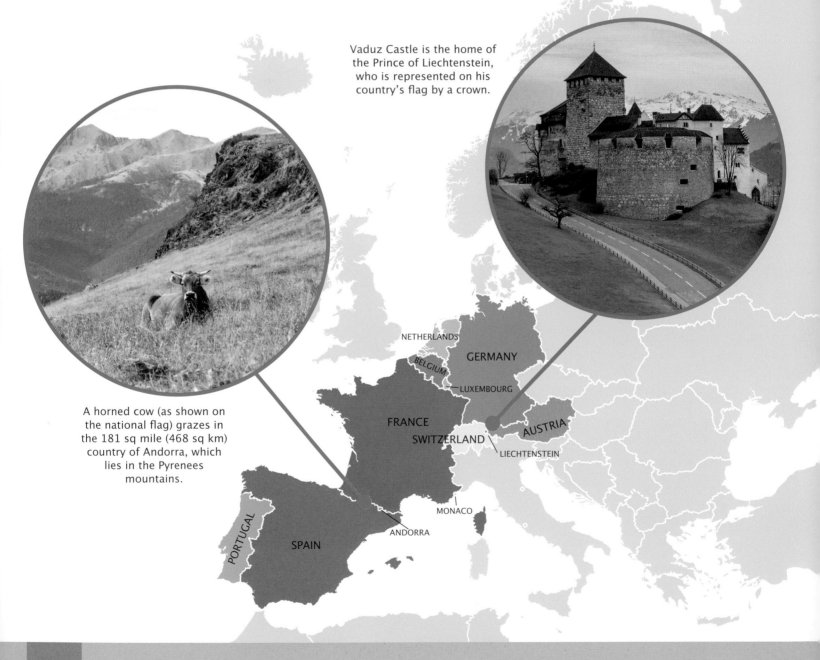

Vaduz Castle is the home of the Prince of Liechtenstein, who is represented on his country's flag by a crown.

A horned cow (as shown on the national flag) grazes in the 181 sq mile (468 sq km) country of Andorra, which lies in the Pyrenees mountains.

NETHERLANDS

BELGIUM

GERMANY

LUXEMBOURG

FRANCE

SWITZERLAND

AUSTRIA

LIECHTENSTEIN

MONACO

ANDORRA

PORTUGAL

SPAIN

NETHERLANDS

Before 1660, the Netherlands flag was orange, white, and blue, based on the coat of arms of William of Orange, who led the fight for independence from Spain in the late 16th century. Today's flag has a proportion of 2:3.

GERMANY

The current black, red, and gold tricolor of Germany was adopted in 1949, having previously been used during periods of both the 19th and early 20th centuries. The flag has a proportion of 3:5.

BELGIUM

The flag of Belgium is nearly square, with a proportion of 13:15. The tricolor was adopted in 1831, based on the colors of the coat of arms of medieval rulers of the region and inspired by the French tricolor.

LUXEMBOURG

Flown since 1848, Luxembourg's flag is similar to that of the Netherlands, but its red and blue are both lighter in shade. The colors are taken from the coat of arms of the royal House of Luxembourg.

FRANCE

The French flag took its colors from the traditional colors of Paris. In 1790, the first tricolor flag was flown, with the stripes ordered red, white, blue. Four years later, the order of the stripes was reversed.

MONACO

Adopted in 1881, the flag of Monaco is a bicolor. Its red and white were taken from the coat of arms of the House of Grimaldi, the monarchs of Monaco since 1297. The flag's proportion is 4:5.

SWITZERLAND

Based on battle flags that had been flown since the 14th century, the flag of Switzerland was officially adopted in 1841. The height of the cross is fixed at 62.5 percent of the height of the flag.

LIECHTENSTEIN

The crown was added to the flag of Liechtenstein in 1937, after officials realized their flag's similarity to the bicolor variant flag of Haiti. Blue represents the sky, while red symbolizes the warmth of home.

AUSTRIA

Flown by Austrian armies from 1230, this flag was most recently readopted in 1945. A legend says the flag was invented by Leopold V of Austria, who found his white battle coat covered by blood, apart from under his belt.

SPAIN

The central stripe of this flag is twice the height of the others, a design known as a "Spanish fess." The Spanish coat of arms features the motto: *Plus ultra* ("Further beyond"), suggesting striving for excellence and knowledge.

ANDORRA

This tricolor is charged with the national coat of arms, which carries the symbols of Andorra's two historical co-princes: the miter (hat) of the Bishop of Urgell and the three vertical red stripes of the Count of Foix.

PORTUGAL

In this bicolor, the green stripe occupies two-fifths of the flag's width. The national coat of arms features an armillary sphere (see page 79) and a shield containing five smaller shields, representing five wounds of Christ.

DID YOU KNOW? The Swiss flag is one of only two national flags that are square, the other belonging to Vatican City.

A Symbol of Freedom

The French flag was first flown during the French Revolution (1789–99). This was when the people of France—many of them poor and hungry—overthrew the king, Louis XVI, and his supporters. Over 16,000 people were executed. The revolutionaries fought for *liberté, égalité, fraternité*: freedom, equality, and brotherhood. Across the world, the French Revolution became a symbol of fairer government, resulting in the French tricolor inspiring the flags of countries across the world, from Italy to Chad.

The revolutionaries often wore cockades, or rosettes of ribbons, in red, white, and blue.

The crown represents the Spanish royal family.

The Spanish flag is known as the *Rojigualda* ("Red–Weld") because of the weld plant that used to provide yellow dye.

A Symbol of Discovery

Behind the shield on the flag of Portugal is a device called an armillary sphere. This was used for navigation by the Portuguese sailors who made extraordinary journeys across the world's oceans from the 15th century. In 1498, Vasco da Gama was the first European to reach India by sea. In 1519, Ferdinand Magellan set off on the first successful voyage around the world. The armillary sphere is a model of the sky, with rings that represent the movement of the Sun and stars. Markers enabled a sailor to plot their rough distance north and south of the equator, as well as east and west.

On the flag of Portugal, the armillary sphere represents Portugal's history and daring.

FLAG FOCUS: Europe

Type: International organization

In use: 1955–present

Flown by: The 27 European countries that are members of the European Union, as well as the 47 countries that are members of the Council of Europe, both of which work for peace, stability, and progress

Design: A circle of 12 golden stars appears on a dark blue background, representing the sky. Although the number of members of the European Union and Council of Europe changes, the number of stars remains fixed, representing the people of Europe joined in peace forever.

DID YOU KNOW? Only three national flags feature farm animals: Andorra (two cows), Bolivia (a llama), and Croatia (a goat).

Southeast Europe

Many of the flags in Southeast Europe feature their country's coat of arms, displaying symbols that represent the country's past rulers, geography, or history. This region is home to Europe's newest national flags, those of Serbia and Montenegro, both adopted in 2004. The region's oldest flag, dating to 1862, belongs to San Marino, one of two small countries that are enclaved (or completely surrounded) by Italy.

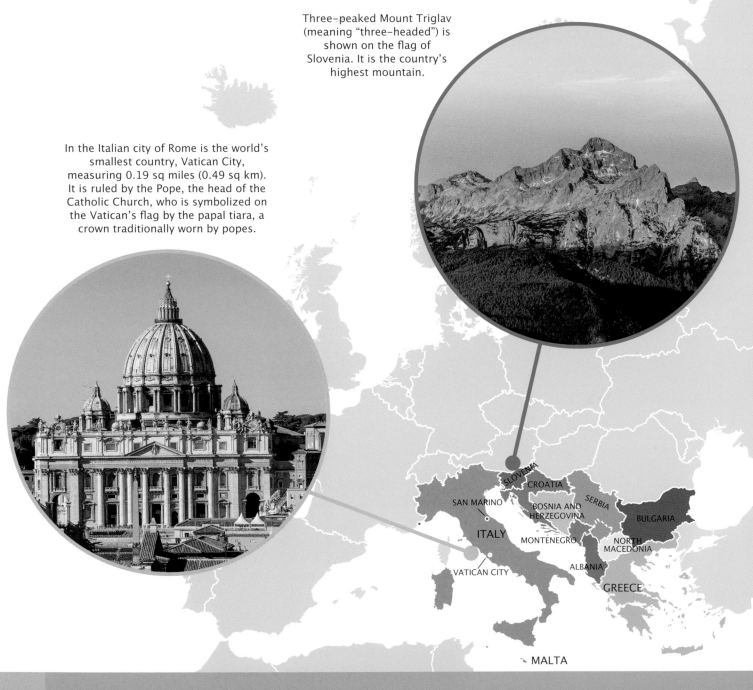

Three-peaked Mount Triglav (meaning "three-headed") is shown on the flag of Slovenia. It is the country's highest mountain.

In the Italian city of Rome is the world's smallest country, Vatican City, measuring 0.19 sq miles (0.49 sq km). It is ruled by the Pope, the head of the Catholic Church, who is symbolized on the Vatican's flag by the papal tiara, a crown traditionally worn by popes.

SLOVENIA
CROATIA
SAN MARINO
BOSNIA AND HERZEGOVINA
SERBIA
BULGARIA
ITALY
MONTENEGRO
NORTH MACEDONIA
VATICAN CITY
ALBANIA
GREECE
MALTA

ITALY

The current Italian design was adopted in 1946, but a green, white, and red flag was first flown by an Italian state in 1789, long before Italy was united in 1870. Today's flag has a proportion of 2:3.

VATICAN CITY

Adopted in 1929, this square flag is a bicolor with the coat of arms of the Holy See (the area where the Pope has authority) and Vatican City. This includes the crossed keys to the kingdom of heaven.

SAN MARINO

The colors of the flag of San Marino symbolize peace (white) and freedom (light blue). At the center is a coat of arms (see page 82) bearing the motto *Libertas* (Freedom).

MALTA

Malta's flag has a depiction of a medal called the George Cross at its upper left corner. The medal was awarded to the island for its bravery during World War II by Britain's King George VI.

SLOVENIA

Adopted in 1991, the Slovenian flag is charged with the national coat of arms, featuring Mount Triglav (see opposite), wavy lines representing the Mediterranean Sea, and three stars, emblems of the medieval counts of the region.

CROATIA

The Croatian flag features the Pan-Slavic colors of red, white, and blue. These colors are used by peoples who speak Slavic languages, found in a region from southeastern Europe to northern Asia.

BOSNIA AND HERZEGOVINA

In this 1998 flag, the three points of the yellow triangle stand for the country's three main peoples: Bosniaks, Croats, and Serbs. The stars (which are cut off at top and bottom, suggesting that they continue forever) represent Europe (see page 79).

SERBIA

A tricolor of the Pan-Slavic colors, the flag of Serbia is charged with the national coat of arms (see page 82). Although Serbia is today a republic, a crown represents the Serbian monarchy.

MONTENEGRO

The flag of Montenegro has a red field, bordered with gold and charged with the national coat of arms (see page 82). The design is based on a 19th-century banner of a prince of Montenegro.

BULGARIA

Bulgaria's tricolor was readopted in 1990. Its white stripe stands for peace and freedom, the green for farming, and the red for bravery and the country's past battle for independence.

ALBANIA

Although a similar design was first flown in 1912, the current flag was adopted in 2002. It features a black two-headed eagle (see page 82) on a blood red field. The red represents bravery, strength, and past battles.

NORTH MACEDONIA

Adopted in 1995, the flag of Macedonia was designed by artist Miroslav Grčev. It features a stylized yellow sun, with eight broadening rays. The sun represents freedom, while also resembling rayed symbols often seen in the region's ancient art.

GREECE

Adopted in 1978, this flag has nine blue and white stripes, said to represent the nine letters in the Greek word for "freedom." The white cross represents Eastern Orthodox Christianity. Blue and white symbolize sea and sky.

DID YOU KNOW? The yellow triangle on the flag of Bosnia and Herzegovina roughly copies the shape of the country.

The Three Towers of San Marino

The flag of San Marino is emblazoned with the country's coat of arms, which depicts three towers on three peaks. These simplified towers represent the three towers on the three peaks of the country's Mount Titano. The towers, named Cesta, Guaita, and Montale, were built as watchtowers from the 11th to 14th centuries. They are visible throughout San Marino. The peaks are also represented in the country's popular dessert, *torta tre monti* ("three mountain cake"), which contains layers of wafers and chocolate or hazelnut cream.

The tower of Guaita watches over the capital of San Marino, also called San Marino.

Double-Headed Eagles

The flags of Albania, Montenegro, and Serbia feature double-headed eagles. As a large bird of prey, the eagle has long been a symbol of strength. The Roman Empire (27 BCE–476 CE) used a single-headed eagle as its symbol. After Rome was conquered, the eastern portion of its empire continued as the Byzantine Empire (395–1453 CE), centered on the city of Constantinople (today Istanbul), in modern Turkey. At times, the empire included the regions of Albania, Montenegro, and Serbia. Byzantine rulers adopted a double-headed eagle as their symbol. They may have been influenced by ancient Turkish carvings, which show double-headed eagles as god-like and all-seeing. In the Middle Ages, the symbol was adopted by ruling families in Albania, Montenegro, and Serbia.

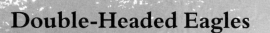

A double-headed eagle decorates a garden fence in Albania.

DID YOU KNOW? The Croatian flag features a pine marten (*kuna* in Croatian) since their skins were once used as money in the region. Today, Croatia's currency is called the kuna.

Type: Region

In use: 2000–present

Flown by: The Italian island of Sicily

Design: The flag is charged with a triskelion (see also page 69), or three bent legs, with the head of Medusa, a mythological creature who could turn people to stone with a stare. This Sicilian symbol dates back to at least the 4th century BCE, when it was used on coins. The head of Medusa drives away evil, while the three legs represent the island's roughly triangular shape.

The Greek flag is raised in Athens near the Parthenon temple, which dates from the 5th century BCE.

A member of the Presidential Guard, an Evzone soldier wears a traditional kilt.

East Europe

In this region, the majority of flags are simple tricolors or bicolors, with three or two stripes. Of all the world's national flags, only four are pure bicolors, without any other pattern or symbol: Indonesia, Monaco, Poland, and Ukraine. The last two are in this region, the simple designs showcasing their country's national colors, which date back to the banners waved during medieval battles.

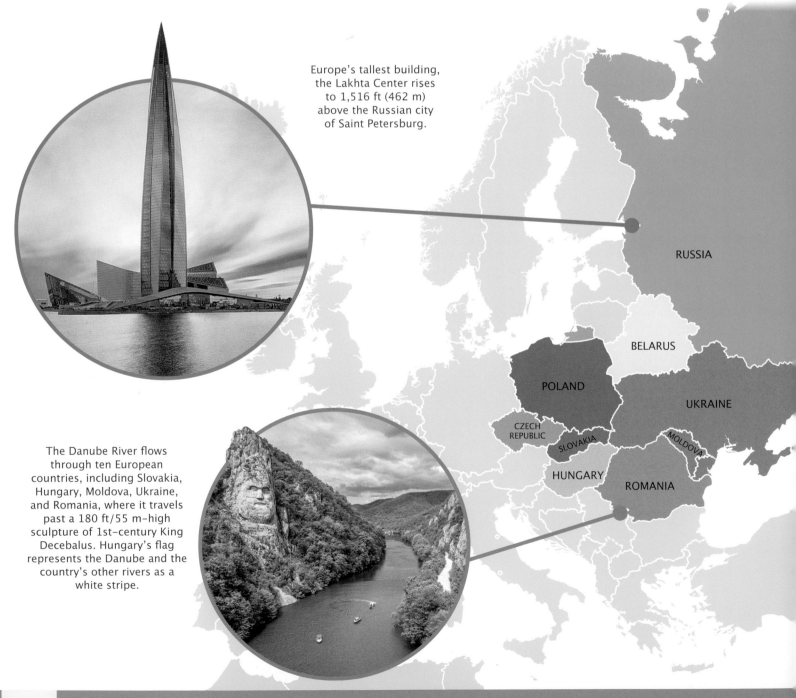

Europe's tallest building, the Lakhta Center rises to 1,516 ft (462 m) above the Russian city of Saint Petersburg.

The Danube River flows through ten European countries, including Slovakia, Hungary, Moldova, Ukraine, and Romania, where it travels past a 180 ft/55 m–high sculpture of 1st-century King Decebalus. Hungary's flag represents the Danube and the country's other rivers as a white stripe.

RUSSIA

BELARUS

POLAND

UKRAINE

CZECH REPUBLIC

SLOVAKIA

MOLDOVA

HUNGARY

ROMANIA

DID YOU KNOW? The pattern along the hoist side of the Belarus flag is taken from a *rushnyk*, a traditional embroidered cloth used during weddings and funerals.

POLAND

Poland's bicolor displays the national colors, which have been seen on royal banners since the Middle Ages. In the 14th century, the royal banner of King Vladislaus the Elbow-High was a red cloth emblazoned with a white eagle. Today's flag design was officially adopted in 1919, although the current shade of red and proportion (5:8) was not specified until 1980.

BELARUS

The flag of Belarus was adopted in 1995, although its design was slightly modified in 2012. The bicolor's red stripe is twice the height of the green stripe. Red represents freedom and past military battles. Green stands for the country's forests and fields, spring and hope, and life itself. A traditional ornamental design is displayed along the hoist.

RUSSIA

Inspired by the flag of the Netherlands, the flag of Russia inspired several other countries in southeastern and eastern Europe to adopt its colors (today known as the Pan-Slavic colors) to represent their Slavic peoples. Many Russians also identify the colors as symbolizing honesty (white), loyalty (blue), and courage (red).

CZECH REPUBLIC

Before 1993, this flag represented the country of Czechoslovakia, which then divided into the Czech Republic and Slovakia. Until 1920, the flag was a simple white and red bicolor, but the blue chevron was then added to distinguish the design from Poland's flag and to display all the Pan-Slavic colors. The flag's proportion is 2:3.

SLOVAKIA

This flag was adopted in 1992, shortly before Slovakia became an independent state on January 1, 1993. To differentiate the tricolor from Russia's flag, it is charged with the national coat of arms (see page 86). This features a double cross, with two horizontal bars, which may represent the death (top bar) and rebirth (bottom bar) of Jesus.

UKRAINE

The flag of Ukraine is a bicolor, with the blue stripe representing the sky and the yellow representing wheat, the country's major crop. Together, the stripes create a simplified picture of the Ukrainian landscape. The colors were first used in medieval battle standards of the region. The flag was readopted as the national flag in 1992.

HUNGARY

With a proportion of 1:2, the flag of Hungary is a tricolor of red, white, and green. The colors were taken from the 15th-century Hungarian coat of arms, while the triband design was inspired by the French flag, as a symbol of freedom. The flag was first flown widely during the Hungarian Revolution of 1848, a rebellion against the Austrian Empire.

ROMANIA

The flag of Romania was readopted in 1989, having first been flown in the mid-19th century. Today, the colors symbolize liberty (blue), justice (yellow), and togetherness (red). The flag of the president of Romania is a square tricolor with the addition of a border, while the naval flag is charged with crossed anchors.

MOLDOVA

Adopted in 1990, the flag of Moldova shares its colors with neighboring Romania, but has the addition of the national coat of arms on the central stripe. This features an eagle, holding a cross (representing Eastern Orthodox Christianity) in its beak and an olive branch (for peace) and scepter (a symbol of past rulers of the region) in its talons.

Three Mountains for Slovakia

The coat of arms on Slovakia's flag features three mountains, which represent three mountain ranges: Tatra, Fatra, and Matra. While the Tatra and Fatra are within the borders of Slovakia, the Matra is in neighboring Hungary. The three hills were first seen in the seal of King Stephen V, who ruled the whole region in the 13th century. A seal was a device used for pressing a symbol into the wax used to close documents.

Reaching a height of 8,711 ft (2,655 m), the Tatras are home to brown bears, wolves, and wild boar.

Russia celebrates its national flag day on August 22.

FLAG FOCUS: Zheleznogorsk

Type: City

In use: 2012–present

Flown by: Zheleznogorsk, Russia

Design: On a red field is a yellow bear, encircled by three white rings, representing the movement of tiny particles called electrons around the center of an atom, called a nucleus. Atoms are the smallest part of any material that can exist. The bear is ripping a nucleus, representing the town's nuclear industry, which releases energy for electricity by splitting nuclei. Russia's national animal is the Eurasian brown bear.

Three Times for Russia

Many current national flags have had a period when an alternative flag was used, before they were readopted. The Russian flag is one of the only national flags that has been readopted twice. The current white, blue, and red tricolor was in use by 1700, before being replaced with a black, yellow, and white tricolor in 1858. The original tricolor was readopted in 1896, before being replaced in 1918 after the Russian Revolution, when Russia's ruler, Tsar Nicholas II, was overthrown. From 1922 to 1991, Russia and 14 other countries were part of the Soviet Union, flying a flag that featured a hammer and sickle, which are tools used by industrial and farming workers. The tricolor was readopted in 1991.

> **Most Russians agree that the red stripe stands for courage and love.**

A worker sews the Russian flag at a factory in Moscow, Russia's capital.

DID YOU KNOW? The Moldova flag features the head of an aurochs, an animal that was related to modern cows but became extinct in the 17th century.

The United States

Also known as the Stars and Stripes, the flag of the United States was first flown in 1777, making it the oldest national flag in the Americas. Each of the country's 50 states also flies its own flag. The newest is the flag of Mississippi, which was redesigned in 2021. The flag of Texas was the first to be officially adopted with its current design, back in 1839.

An American bison is emblazoned on the state flag of Wyoming, as well as featuring in the state seal on the Kansas flag. Bison hunting was central to the lives of Native Americans for thousands of years before the arrival of Europeans. Today, the bison is found in only a few preserves, including Yellowstone National Park.

UNITED STATES
OF AMERICA

The Hudson River appears on the flag of New York state, as a symbol of the trade that made the region wealthy. The Hudson flows past New York's Manhattan Island, which is home to One World Trade Center, the tallest building in the United States at 1,776 ft (541 m).

WASHINGTON
MONTANA
NORTH DAKOTA
MINNESOTA
VERMONT
MAINE
NEW HAMPSHIRE
OREGON
IDAHO
SOUTH DAKOTA
WISCONSIN
NEW YORK
MASSACHUSETTS
RHODE ISLAND
WYOMING
MICHIGAN
PENNSYLVANIA
CONNECTICUT
NEVADA
NEBRASKA
IOWA
INDIANA
OHIO
NEW JERSEY
DELAWARE
UTAH
ILLINOIS
WEST VIRGINIA
MARYLAND
CALIFORNIA
COLORADO
KANSAS
MISSOURI
KENTUCKY
VIRGINIA
ARIZONA
NEW MEXICO
OKLAHOMA
ARKANSAS
TENNESSEE
NORTH CAROLINA
SOUTH CAROLINA
MISSISSIPPI
ALABAMA
GEORGIA
TEXAS
LOUISIANA
FLORIDA
ALASKA
HAWAII

UNITED STATES

The Stars and Stripes has 13 horizontal red and white stripes, with 50 white stars on a blue rectangle in the upper left corner (see page 90). The flag has the unusual proportion of 10:19, based on the standard size of cloth rolls in the 18th century.

States

Alabama	Alaska	Arizona	Arkansas	California	Colorado	Connecticut
Delaware	Florida	Georgia	Hawaii	Idaho	Illinois	Indiana
Iowa	Kansas	Kentucky	Louisiana	Maine	Maryland	Massachusetts
Michigan	Minnesota	Mississippi	Missouri	Montana	Nebraska	Nevada
New Hampshire	New Jersey	New Mexico	New York	North Carolina	North Dakota	Ohio
Oklahoma	Oregon	Pennsylvania	Rhode Island	South Carolina	South Dakota	Tennessee
Texas	Utah	Vermont	Virginia	Washington	West Virginia	
Wisconsin	Wyoming					

DID YOU KNOW? The US flag was designed by judge and composer Francis Hopkinson, one of the 56 men who signed the 1776 Declaration of Independence.

The Stars and Stripes

When the US flag was first raised, on June 14, 1777, it featured 13 white, five-pointed stars on a blue rectangle, with 13 red-and-white stripes, both representing the 13 American colonies that had declared independence from Great Britain on July 4, 1776 and became the first states in the United States. The flag has since been modified 26 times as new stars were added following each state's admission to the union. Since 1960, the flag has had 50 stars, after Hawaii gained statehood the previous year.

On July 4, Americans celebrate Independence Day with parades and parties.

Flying the 13-starred flag, American forces accept the British surrender at Yorktown in 1781.

FLAG FOCUS: Denver

Type: City

In use: 1926-present

Flown by: Denver, capital of the US state of Colorado

Design: The design represents a yellow sun in a blue sky, rising above red snow-capped mountains. The red of the mountains refers to the red-colored earth that gave the state its name, which means "colored red" in Spanish. At a height of over 4,920 ft (1,500 m) above sea level, Denver is in the foothills of the Rocky Mountains.

DID YOU KNOW? Oregon is the only US state with a two-sided flag, the reverse of which shows the state's official animal, the beaver.

The flag's red symbolizes courage, white stands for innocence, and blue for justice.

The Bald Eagle

Eight flags of US states feature an eagle: Illinois, Iowa, Michigan, New York, North Dakota, Oregon, Pennsylvania, and Utah. Eagles have been associated with power since Roman times (see page 82). Found across North America, the bald eagle is the national bird. It can be seen on the Great Seal of the United States, which has been used to prove the authenticity of government documents since 1782. On the seal, the eagle holds 13 arrows in one talon, with an olive branch with 13 leaves and 13 olives in the other. These objects represent war and peace. The eagle has its face turned toward the olive branch, showing the country's desire for peace but its willingness to defend itself.

The Great Seal shows an eagle holding a ribbon that bears the 13–letter motto: *E pluribus unum* (Out of many, one). This refers to the fact that one nation emerged from the 13 original colonies.

Canada

The flag of Canada, known as *l'Unifolié* (the "one-leafed") in French, is charged with a maple leaf. Canada's ten provinces and three territories fly their own flags alongside the national flag. Seven of those flags also feature plants: maple leaves, oak trees, wheat, fireweed, a prairie lily, and fleurs-de-lis, a design based on an iris flower.

The Arctic fox, seen on the flag of Northwest Territories, does not start to shiver until the temperature falls to –94°F (–70°C) thanks to its thick fur, which even covers the soles of its feet.

With its pink blooms, fireweed is the floral emblem of the Canadian territory of Yukon. Yukon is the least populated of all Canada's territories or provinces, with an average of 0.08 people living in each 0.4 sq miles (1 sq km).

CANADA

YUKON

NORTHWEST TERRITORIES

NUNAVUT

BRITISH COLUMBIA

ALBERTA

SASKATCHEWAN

MANITOBA

ONTARIO

QUEBEC

NEWFOUNDLAND AND LABRADOR

PRINCE EDWARD ISLAND

NEW BRUNSWICK

NOVA SCOTIA

CANADA

With a proportion of 1:2, the flag of Canada features an 11-pointed maple leaf (see page 95) in a white square, which is centered in a red field. Red represents hope and happiness, while white is for peace.

Provinces and Territories

Alberta
Adopted in 1968, this flag is charged with the province's coat of arms, which depicts the Rocky Mountains, prairie grasslands, and wheat fields.

British Columbia
This flag displays the Union Jack, reflecting the province's British history. Behind a setting sun are wavy lines representing the ocean and mountains.

Manitoba
Based on the Red Ensign flown by British merchant ships, this flag displays a bison, which formerly roamed the province in large herds.

New Brunswick
Based on the province's coat of arms, this flag features a lymphad, a sailing ship propelled by oars, representing the ship-building industry.

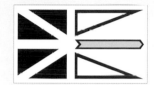

Newfoundland and Labrador
Designed in 1980 by artist Christopher Pratt, this flag echoes both the Union Jack and jewelry worn by the province's indigenous peoples.

Northwest Territories
This flag represents the territory's landscape: blue for the Arctic Ocean, white for ice, green for the southern trees, and red for icy, treeless tundra.

Nova Scotia
Based on Scotland's St Andrew's Cross and charged with Scotland's royal arms, this flag reflects the province's many Scottish settlers.

Nunavut
This 1999 flag is charged with a red *inuksuk* (see page 94) and a blue star, representing the North Star and the wisdom of community leaders.

Ontario
Adopted in 1965, the flag of Ontario is based on the Red Ensign. In the fly, the province's coat of arms depicts three gold maple leaves.

Prince Edward Island
Three oak saplings symbolize the province's three counties, under a tree representing Britain. Apart from the hoist, the edges of the flag are bordered.

Quebec
This flag reflects the province's French heritage through the use of four fleurs-de-lis, symbols often seen on the flags of French kings.

Saskatchewan
The yellow stripe stands for the province's southern fields of grain, while the green stripe symbolizes the northern forests. A prairie lily is in the fly.

Yukon
The territory's coat of arms rests on a wreath of fireweed. The green stripe symbolizes forests, the white is for snow, and the blue signifies rivers.

DID YOU KNOW? A symbol of royal purity, the fleur-de-lis was used by French kings from at least as early as 1060 and today appears on two national flags: Serbia and Spain.

The Inuksuk

The flag of the Canadian territory of Nunavut is charged with a red *inuksuk* (plural: *inuksuit*). Traditionally, *inuksuit* are built by the Inuit and other peoples of the Arctic regions of North America. In these regions, where it is too cold for trees to grow, there are few natural landmarks. *Inuksuit*, built from stones, were placed to mark the location of hunting routes, fishing spots, and camp grounds. Today, *inuksuit* are a symbol of Inuit culture and, more and more, a symbol of all Canadians.

In the Inuit language Inuktitut, *inuksuk* means "to act like a human."

A maple leaf is a palmate leaf, with several pointed leaflets spreading from its center.

DID YOU KNOW? The setting sun on the flag of British Columbia represents the province's position on the western (sunset) side of Canada.

As it gets colder in the fall, maple leaves turn yellow to red, then drop from the tree.

The Maple Leaf

The maple leaf on the Canadian national flag represents the ten different species of maples, all with slightly different leaves, that grow in forests across southern Canada. Long before the arrival of Europeans, Canada's First Nations were collecting sweet maple sap to make syrup. Today, the syrup is used as a baking ingredient or drizzled on pancakes and waffles. The maple leaf was first adopted as an emblem by French Canadians in the early 18th century. By 1868, maple leaves were emblazoned on the coats of arms of Ontario and Quebec. The leaf appeared on all Canadian coins from 1876, before being adopted on the national flag in 1965.

Holes are drilled in a maple trunk to release sap, a sticky liquid rich in sugar made by the tree.

FLAG FOCUS:
Council of the Haida Nation

Type: Region

In use: 1974–present

Flown by: The elected government of the Haida Nation, who traditionally live on the islands of Haida Gwaii, off the coast of Canada's British Columbia

Design: At the center of the flag is a depiction of a traditional wooden carving in a style often seen in Haida totem poles, which display ancestors, events, and stories. The two birds represent the two Haida family groups, the Ravens and the Eagles.

Mexico and Central America

Four Central American countries—El Salvador, Guatemala, Honduras, and Nicaragua—have triband flags, with blue, white, and blue stripes. Along with Costa Rica, these countries formed the Federal Republic of Central America (1823–41) and base their designs on the flag of that country, which was itself based on the flag of Argentina (see page 105). The stripes of blue also represent the two oceans, Pacific and Atlantic, that border the strip of land on which Central America lies.

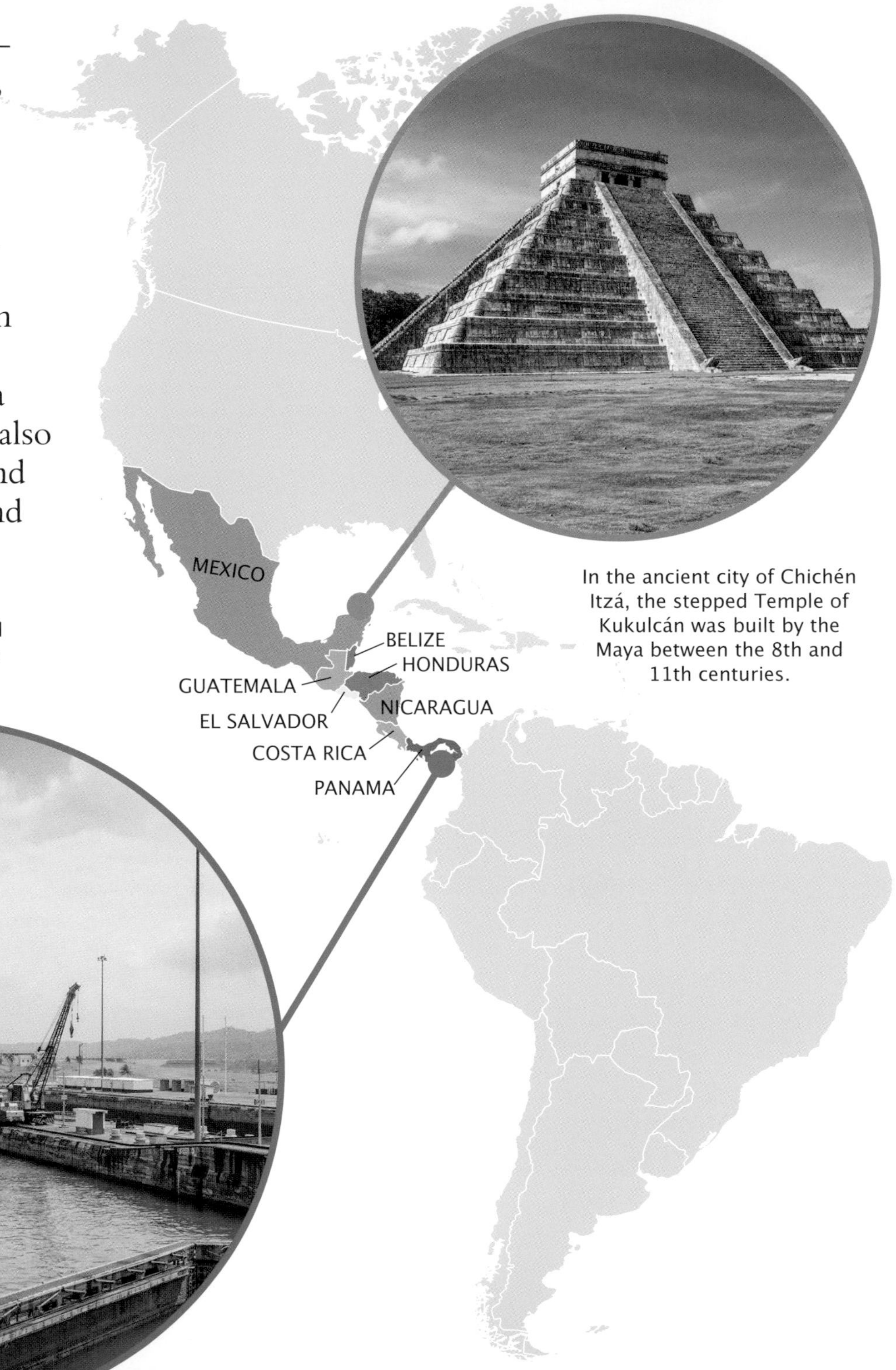

The 51-mile (82-km), human-made Panama Canal cuts across Panama, providing a shortcut between the Atlantic and Pacific Oceans.

MEXICO
BELIZE
HONDURAS
GUATEMALA
EL SALVADOR
NICARAGUA
COSTA RICA
PANAMA

In the ancient city of Chichén Itzá, the stepped Temple of Kukulcán was built by the Maya between the 8th and 11th centuries.

MEXICO

The colors of the Mexican flag were adopted in 1821, when the country gained independence from Spain. Green represents independence, white is for the Catholic Church, and red for unity. Although the exact design of the central coat of arms (see page 98) has changed several times since 1821, most recently in 1968, its emblems have remained the same.
The flag has a proportion of 4:7.

GUATEMALA

Adopted in 1871, the blue and white stripes of Guatemala's flag are described in the national anthem: "Your emblem is a piece of the sky/ From which a cloud gets its whiteness..." In the center is the national coat of arms, featuring a resplendent quetzal (see page 98), rifles (see page 99), and swords. A parchment bears the date of independence from Spain: September 15, 1821.

BELIZE

The only national flag to feature humans as a central design element, the 1981 flag of Belize depicts two woodcutters, holding an ax and paddle, and a mahogany tree, all representing the importance of mahogany wood in Belize's history. On a scroll, the national motto, *Sub Umbra Floreo* (Under the shade I flourish), also refers to the country's forests.

EL SALVADOR

Adopted in 1912, the flag of El Salvador features the national coat of arms between two stripes of cobalt blue. The arms feature a liberty cap (see page 106); five volcanoes, representing the five members of the Federal Republic of Central America; a rainbow, symbolizing peace; four national flags; and a scroll with the country's motto: *Dios, Unión, Libertad* (God, Union, Liberty).

HONDURAS

The flag of Honduras was adopted in 1866, although it has since had minor changes. The five, five-pointed stars symbolize the nations of the former Federal Republic of Central America. In addition to representing the oceans, the two blue stripes stand for the sky and togetherness. The white stripe represents the land between the oceans, the people of Honduras, and pure thoughts.

NICARAGUA

First flown in 1908, Nicaragua's flag is charged with the national coat of arms, which is very similar to El Salvador's and based on the arms of the former Federal Republic of Central America. The triangular shape of the emblem represents the three branches of government: executive (enforcing laws), legislative (making laws), and judiciary (interpreting the meaning of laws).

COSTA RICA

The Costa Rica flag has stripes of blue (for sky, hope, and effort), white (for peace, happiness, and wisdom), and red (for past battles, bravery, and generosity), with the red stripe double the height of the other stripes.
The flag is charged with the national coat of arms, featuring three smoking volcanoes, representing the country's three mountain ranges.
The flag was adopted in 1906.

PANAMA

The flag of Panama is divided into quarters, representing the rival political parties of the period when the design was created, in 1903. Red was for the Liberals and blue for the Conservatives, joined together by white, representing peace. The flag was sketched by the family of the first president of Panama, Manuel Amador Guerrero, when the country broke away from Colombia.

DID YOU KNOW? The Belize flag has the most colors of any national flag, 12, the majority appearing in its coat of arms.

97

The Eagle and the Cactus

At the center of Mexico's flag is a golden eagle, which perches on a prickly pear cactus and devours a rattlesnake. A legend tells that, in the 14th century, the Mexica people were wandering in the Valley of Mexico. The sun god Huitzilopochtli had told them to live on the spot where they saw an eagle eating prey on a cactus. Finally, they saw an eagle doing just that on an island in Lake Texcoco. This was where they founded their city, Tenochtitlan, which grew into the capital of the Aztec empire and today's Mexico City. To the Mexica, the eagle represented the sun god, while the snake represented the serpent god Quetzalcoatl. To later generations, the symbol came to represent the triumph of good over evil.

The legend is depicted on the first page of the *Codex Mendoza*, a book created by Aztec artists in around 1541.

Appearing on the country's flag, the resplendent quetzal is the national bird of Guatemala.

DID YOU KNOW? The flag of Costa Rica is one of seven national flags that include a depiction of the national flag itself.

Type: City

In use: 2006–present

Flown by: San José, the capital of Costa Rica

Design: The flag is divided into horizontal bands of blue, green, and white, in the proportion of 5:1:1 (the green and white bands are each one–fifth the height of the blue band). The 11 white stars represent the 11 districts of the city. Blue represents the sky, green stands for the land and for hope, and white is for honesty.

Prized by the Aztecs and Maya, its long green tail feathers are symbols of liberty, light, and growth.

The Rifles of Guatemala

The flag of Guatemala is one of four national flags that feature firearms. While the Bolivian and Haitian flags both feature canons and rifles, the flag of Mozambique depicts an AK-47 rifle. Guatemala's crossed Remington rifles represent the nation's willingness to defend itself. The rifles have appeared in the national coat of arms since the 1871 revolution, when the government was overthrown and improvements were made to education, trade, and transport.

On September 15, Guatemalans celebrate the day in 1821 when the region declared independence from Spain.

The Caribbean

The more than 700 islands of the Caribbean Sea are home to 13 countries, each with its own national flag. Many of these flags represent the region's natural wonders and riches, from volcanic peaks to plants, animals, and the ocean. There are also 17 dependencies and constituent countries in the Caribbean, which form part of countries including France and the Netherlands (see page 116).

With a population of 2.9 million people, the Dominican Republic's Santo Domingo is the largest city in the Caribbean.

The twin Pitons peaks, created when molten rock hardened in the necks of volcanoes, are represented on the national flag of St. Lucia.

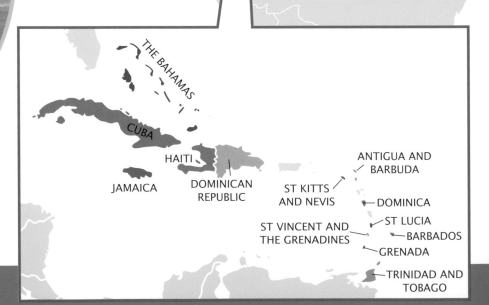

THE BAHAMAS

CUBA

HAITI

JAMAICA

DOMINICAN REPUBLIC

ST KITTS AND NEVIS

ANTIGUA AND BARBUDA

DOMINICA

ST LUCIA

ST VINCENT AND THE GRENADINES

BARBADOS

GRENADA

TRINIDAD AND TOBAGO

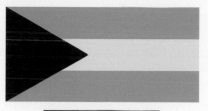

THE BAHAMAS

Adopted in 1973, the Bahamas' flag symbolizes the ocean (aquamarine), the sun (yellow), and the strength of Bahamian people (black). The arrow-like triangle suggests determination.

CUBA

The three blue stripes represent the three original regions of Cuba. The colors of red, white, and blue were inspired by the French flag, seen as a symbol of fair government. The flag was designed in 1849 and adopted in 1902.

JAMAICA

Featuring a yellow saltire, the 1962 flag of Jamaica uses its colors to represent the strength of its people (black), the country's wealth and sunshine (yellow), and the island's lush plants and hope (green).

HAITI

A bicolor of blue and red, the flag of Haiti is charged with the country's coat of arms in a white square. This features a royal palm topped with a liberty cap (see page 106), weapons (see page 99), and six national flags.

DOMINICAN REPUBLIC

The white cross represents Christianity, while the blue rectangles stand for liberty and the red for the blood of heroes. At the center is the national coat of arms, featuring a Bible, laurel branch, and palm frond.

ST KITTS AND NEVIS

The two stars on the flag of St. Kitts and Nevis symbolize the country's two islands. Green represents the plant-covered land, yellow the sun, black the people's African origins, and red the fight against slavery.

ANTIGUA AND BARBUDA

This flag was designed in 1967 by artist Sir Reginald Samuel. The flag's V shape is a symbol of victory, while the rising sun represents hope and progress. The blue signifies the sea and the white is for sand.

DOMINICA

Dominica's flag features a cross, representing Christianity, its three colors standing for the country's people, soil, and water. At the center is a sisserou parrot (see page 102), with 10 stars for Dominica's 10 parishes.

ST LUCIA

Adopted in 1967, the flag of St Lucia uses yellow and black triangles to represent the Pitons (see opposite). The flag's black and white symbolize harmony between the country's peoples.

ST VINCENT AND THE GRENADINES

This 1985 flag is charged with three green diamonds, forming a V, standing for the V of Vincent. In addition, the diamonds refer to the islands' nickname of "Gems of the Caribbean."

BARBADOS

This flag was adopted in 1966, when Barbados gained independence. It features stripes of blue (representing ocean and sky) and a yellow stripe (signifying sand) containing a trident (see page 102).

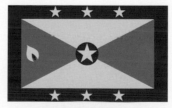

GRENADA

The 1974 flag of Grenada uses the Pan-African colors (see page 32) to represent its people's African heritage. At the hoist is a nutmeg, a key crop on the island that has earned its nickname of "Spice Island."

TRINIDAD AND TOBAGO

Designed when the country gained independence in 1962, this flag uses red, black, and white to symbolize the elements of fire, earth, and water.

DID YOU KNOW? Jamaica's is the only national flag in the world that does not include red, white, or blue in its design.

The Sisserou Parrot

Dominica's flag features its national bird, the sisserou parrot. Found only on the island of Dominica, the sisserou is critically endangered, with fewer than 50 wild birds remaining. Sisserous are at risk of extinction because of the loss of their forest habitat, due to hurricanes and the cutting down of trees for timber and farmland. These loyal birds stay with one mate for life. They feed on fruits, nuts, and seeds.

The sisserou is a symbol of love and loyalty.

The Broken Trident

The flag of Barbados is charged with the head of a three-pronged weapon known as a trident, which has been snapped from its staff. The trident is taken from the island's badge during the time it was ruled by Great Britain, from 1625 to 1966. In this design, a figure of a woman known as Britannia represents Great Britain. She holds a trident, which was linked with the ancient Greek god of the sea, Poseidon. The trident represented the power of Britain's navy, which had enabled Britain to take control of a large empire. The trident on Barbados's flag is broken to show that Barbados is no longer ruled by a foreign power. In addition, the three prongs represent the three principles of democracy, a system of government in which people cast votes to elect their representatives: government of the people, government for the people, and government by the people.

In Barbados's old badge, trident–carrying Britannia rides on "seahorses."

The Broken Trident has been the flag of Barbados since 1966.

The design, by teacher Grantley Prescod, was chosen from 1,029 competition entries.

FLAG FOCUS:
Prime Minister of the Bahamas

Type: Prime Ministerial

In use: 1973–present

Flown by: The residence and car of the prime minister

Design: This flag is the same as the national flag but has a gold and aquamarine parliamentary mace vertically in the fly (opposite to the hoist side). The mace is an ornamented staff that represents the authority of the elected members of parliament.

DID YOU KNOW? Only two national flags include purple: Dominica (the sisserou's plumage) and Nicaragua (as a stripe in its rainbow).

South America

South America is home to 12 countries, as well as French Guiana, a territory of France which flies the French flag. The life-giving sun is represented in six South American flags. It is emblazoned large on the flags of Argentina and Uruguay, appears in the coats of arms of Bolivia and Ecuador, and is symbolized by the color yellow in the flags of Colombia and Venezuela.

The Amazon is the world's largest rain forest, covering 2.1 million sq miles (5.5 million sq km) of South America. Around a hundred species of monkeys live in the forest, including the emperor tamarin.

Bolivia's La Paz is the world's highest capital city, sitting at a height of 11,975 ft (3,650 m) in the Andes Mountains.

VENEZUELA
GUYANA
SURINAME
FRENCH GUIANA
COLOMBIA
ECUADOR
PERU
BRAZIL
BOLIVIA
PARAGUAY
CHILE
ARGENTINA
URUGUAY

DID YOU KNOW? Appearing on Bolivia's flag, the llama is the country's national animal, while its close relative, the vicuña, appears on the variant flag of Peru.

COLOMBIA

Like the flags of Venezuela and Ecuador, this flag is based on the flag of Gran Colombia, a state that covered northern South America from 1819 to 1831.The yellow stripe is twice the height of the blue and red stripes.

VENEZUELA

This tricolor's yellow represents the sun, wealth, and justice; the blue stands for the Caribbean Sea; and the red signifies the blood spilt in the struggle for independence from Spain. Eight stars stand for eight provinces.

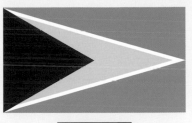

GUYANA

Known as the Golden Arrowhead, the design of the Guyana flag symbolizes progress. Its red stands for effort, black for endurance, yellow for mineral wealth, white for rivers, and green for forests and farming.

SURINAME

Suriname's flag was adopted in 1975. It features stripes of green (for the land), white (for freedom and justice), and red (for progress). The yellow star expresses the country's hope for a golden future.

ECUADOR

Ecuador's flag is identical to Colombia's, but it bears the national coat of arms. This features an Andean condor, the country's Mount Chimborazo, and a river with a steamship, a symbol of trade.

PERU

Adopted in 1825 and last modified In 1950, the flag of Peru is a triband that bears different emblems in its white stripe if it is flown by the government or navy. The red represents past struggles, while white stands for peace.

BRAZIL

A blue disk representing a starry sky (see page 107) is divided by a band bearing the country's motto: *Ordem e progresso* (Order and progress). Green and yellow were taken from the colors of the royal houses of Portugal, who ruled the region from 1500.

BOLIVIA

With a proportion of 15:22, the flag of Bolivia Is a tricolor of red (for bravery), yellow (for wealth), and green (for plant life). The central coat of arms features an Andean condor and six national flags.

CHILE

Chile's flag bears a star representing the planet Venus, which is seen in the sky at dawn and is important to the country's Mapuche people. Blue stands for the sky, white for mountain snow, and red for struggle.

PARAGUAY

The 1842 flag of Paraguay was inspired by the French tricolor, seen as a symbol of freedom. At the flag's center is the national coat of arms, featuring a palm and olive branch.

ARGENTINA

First flown in 1818, Argentina's flag features the "Sun of May," representing both the May Revolution of 1810 against Spanish rule and the Inca god of the sun.

URUGUAY

Inspired by the flag of Argentina, Uruguay's flag was adopted in 1828. It features the Sun of May, as well as nine stripes representing the country's nine original departments.

Liberty Caps

The flag of Bolivia features a liberty cap, a symbol also seen in the flags of El Salvador, Haiti, Nicaragua, and the reverse of the Paraguay flag. A similar soft cap was worn by freed slaves in ancient Rome. The cap was often shown being held by the Roman goddess of liberty, called Libertas. In later centuries, the liberty cap became a symbol of the French Revolution (see page 78) and American Revolution (see page 90). When countries in Central and South America fought against European rule in the 18th and 19th centuries, they also adopted the symbol.

The liberty cap became a worldwide symbol of freedom.

The Brazilian flag is waved by dancers in Rio de Janeiro during Carnival, a festival that marks the start of Lent, a period when many Christians give up meat or luxuries.

A Starry Sky

At the center of the Brazilian flag is a blue disk dotted with stars, their positions reflecting the position of the stars in the sky over Brazil's Rio de Janeiro on November 15, 1889, the day on which Brazil's king was overthrown and it became a republic. The 27 white five-pointed stars also represent Brazil's 26 states and its small Federal District, which is home to the capital, Brasília. The Federal District is represented by the South Pole Star, also called Sigma Octantis, the smallest star in the design. The star Spica, the only one above the white band, represents the large state of Pará, which spreads across the equator.

KEY

1 Spica
2 Procyon
3 Two stars in the constellation Hydra
4 Five stars in the constellation Canis Major
5 Five stars in the constellation Southern Cross
6 Canopus
7 Three stars in the constellation Southern Triangle
8 Eight stars in the constellation Scorpius
9 South Pole Star

FLAG FOCUS: Santa Cruz

Type: Province
In use: 2000–present
Flown by: The province of Santa Cruz, in Argentina

Design: With its sun and pale blue field, this flag reflects Argentina's national flag. The white waving lines on dark blue represent the province's ocean coast. Within the sun are a depiction of the Southern Cross and Mount Fitz Roy, which are both emblems of the region's Aónikenk people.

DID YOU KNOW? The Guyana flag was designed by vexillologist Whitney Smith, who also came up with the word "vexillology" from Latin *vexillum* ("flag") and Greek *logia* ("study").

Australasia

The countries of Australia, New Zealand, and Papua New Guinea all fly flags depicting the Southern Cross stars. Australia is divided into six states and three territories, which all (apart from Jervis Bay) fly their own flags in addition to the national flag. In New Zealand, although some cities fly their own flags, there are no regional flags. Both Australia and New Zealand have external territories in the Indian and Pacific Oceans (see page 120).

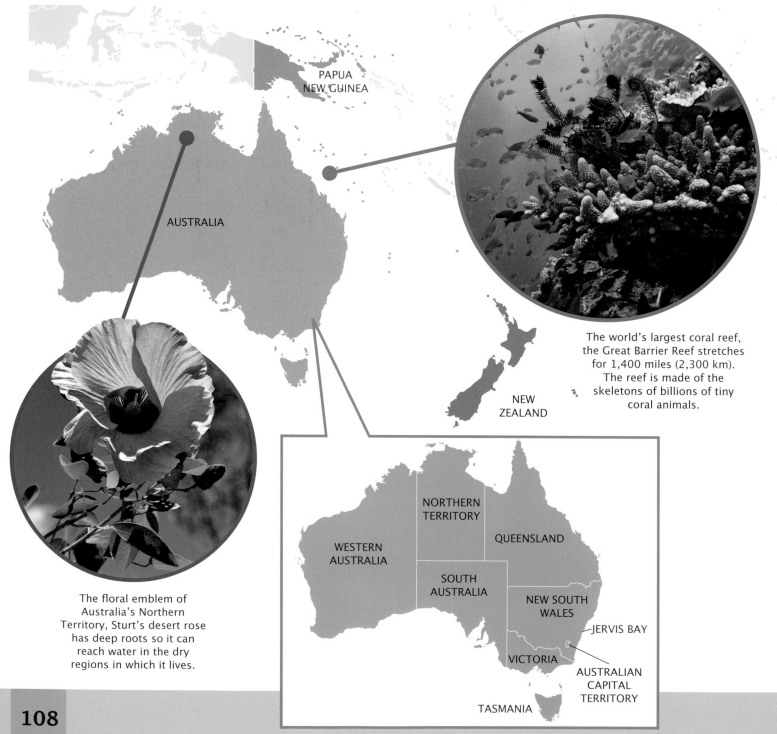

PAPUA
NEW GUINEA

AUSTRALIA

NEW
ZEALAND

The world's largest coral reef, the Great Barrier Reef stretches for 1,400 miles (2,300 km). The reef is made of the skeletons of billions of tiny coral animals.

The floral emblem of Australia's Northern Territory, Sturt's desert rose has deep roots so it can reach water in the dry regions in which it lives.

NORTHERN
TERRITORY

QUEENSLAND

WESTERN
AUSTRALIA

SOUTH
AUSTRALIA

NEW SOUTH
WALES

JERVIS BAY

VICTORIA

AUSTRALIAN
CAPITAL
TERRITORY

TASMANIA

PAPUA NEW GUINEA

Papua New Guinea's flag was designed in 1971 by 15-year-old Susan Karike, who won a national competition. In a black triangle at the hoist is the Southern Cross (see page 110), while in a red triangle is the silhouette of a raggiana bird-of-paradise (see page 110), which is also found in the national coat of arms. Black and red are traditional colors of local peoples. The flag has a proportion of 3:4.

AUSTRALIA

The current design of the Australian flag was first flown in 1908. The Union Jack in the upper left canton reflects the history of British settlement, although many Australians debate whether a more modern design is needed. In the fly is the Southern Cross (see page 110), while below the Union Jack is a seven-pointed star representing the six states and the territories of Australia.

NEW ZEALAND

Like many countries that were or are associated with the United Kingdom, New Zealand flies a flag based on the Blue Ensign: a blue field with a Union Jack in the upper left canton. The fly features the four main stars of the Southern Cross (see page 110). Many New Zealanders question whether the country should adopt a flag that better expresses the country's independence.

States and Internal Territories of Australia

Western Australia
Like the other five states, Western Australia flies a flag based on the Blue Ensign. In the fly is the state badge, featuring a black swan.

Queensland
Queensland's flag, adopted in 1876, features the state's badge in the fly. It depicts a Maltese (with V-shaped arms) cross and imperial crown.

South Australia
South Australia's state badge features a golden sun-like disk with a piping shrike, the unofficial state bird. The flag was adoped in 1904.

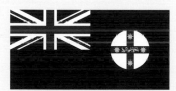

New South Wales
Flown since 1876, this flag features the state's badge of the St. George's Cross and a golden lion, which appears in the arms of England.

Victoria
This flag is the only state flag to feature the Southern Cross. Above it is St. Edward's Crown, part of the United Kingdom's Crown Jewels.

Tasmania
Adopted in 1876, this flag features the state's badge in the fly. It depicts a red lion, representing the state's historical links with the United Kingdom.

Northern Territory
Adopted in 1978, Northern Territory's flag has the Southern Cross on the hoist, with a stylized Sturt's desert rose on a red ocher field.

Australian Capital Territory
Inspired by the Northern Territory's flag, this design was adopted in 1993. The coat of arms of the capital city of Canberra is supported by swans.

DID YOU KNOW? On the Australian Capital Territory's flag, the Australian black swan represents Aboriginal Australians, while the European mute swan is for later settlers.

The Southern Cross

The Southern Cross is emblazoned on the flags of Australia, Brazil, New Zealand, Papua New Guinea, and Samoa. The constellation's four brightest stars form a cross in the southern hemisphere's night sky. For thousands of years, these stars have been used for navigation. In some Aboriginal Australian cultures, the stars and dark sky around them form part of the Emu in the Sky. Traditionally, for New Zealand's Maoris, the stars are the anchor of our galaxy, the Milky Way, which can be seen as a bright streak of stars. For later, Christian settlers, the stars were a symbol of the cross on which Jesus died.

The Southern Cross is mentioned in the national anthems of Australia and Samoa.

The New Zealand rugby team sings the national anthem before a match.

A male shows off his feathers to a watching female, who has darker and shorter plumage.

The Raggiana Bird-of-Paradise

The flag of Papua New Guinea features the silhouette of a male raggiana bird-of-paradise, the country's national bird. This beautiful bird lives only in the tropical forests of eastern New Guinea. To attract females, male raggianas perform dances that show off their long feathers. Local people use these feathers to decorate headdresses worn during traditional dances.

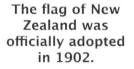

The flag of New Zealand was officially adopted in 1902.

FLAG FOCUS: Tino Rangatiratanga

Type: Cultural or ethnic group

In use: 1990–present

Flown by: New Zealand's Maori community, as well as New Zealand's government buildings and landmarks on national day

Design: The Maori flag is known as Tino Rangatiratanga ("Highest Chieftainship"). The flag displays the national Maori colors: black (representing what can possibly be), red (what is coming into being), and white (what is). The design symbolizes an uncurling fern frond, representing new life and hope.

DID YOU KNOW? In 2015, New Zealanders voted on replacing their flag's Union Jack with a silver fern, a plant found only in New Zealand, but 56 percent wanted to keep the old flag.

Pacific Islands

The Pacific Ocean island groups of Melanesia, Micronesia, and Polynesia are home to 11 countries, as well as several dependent territories (see page 120). Stars or the sun feature on most flags of Pacific Islands. Hundreds or thousands of years ago, these islands were settled by seafarers who navigated using the position of the stars, sun, and ocean swells.

With a population of 271, Palau's Ngerulmud is the world's least populated national capital.

PALAU

FEDERATED STATES OF MICRONESIA

MARSHALL ISLANDS

NAURU

KIRIBATI

SOLOMON ISLANDS

TUVALU

SAMOA

VANUATU

FIJI

TONGA

Vanuatu's only native mammals are bats, but settlers brought pigs with them. The tusks of a male pig are worn as jewelry during traditional ceremonies and appear on the national flag.

PALAU

The yellow disk, positioned to the left of center, represents the full moon, which Palauans see as the best time for harvesting, fishing, carving canoes, and festivals. The blue field signifies the ocean. The flag was adopted in 1981.

FEDERATED STATES OF MICRONESIA

The four stars, arranged like the points of a compass, represent the country's four states. The blue field, the same shade as the United Nations' flag, represents the ocean.

MARSHALL ISLANDS

The flag of the Marshall Islands was designed in 1979 by Emlain Kabua, the wife of the republic's first president. The diagonal stripes represent the equator (see page 114) as well as the sunrise and sunset.

NAURU

Adopted in 1968, this flag features a 12-pointed star, representing the nation's 12 tribes. Divided into two halves, the flag also symbolizes the traditional belief that Nauru's people were born from two boulders.

KIRIBATI

Kiribati's flag depicts a frigatebird (see page 115) above a rising sun, with 17 rays to represent 17 islands. The three white wavy stripes in the ocean stand for the country's three main island groups.

SOLOMON ISLANDS

The five stars in the upper left corner represent the country's original five provinces. Green represents the land and its crops, yellow the sun, and blue the Pacific Ocean and life-giving rivers and rain.

TUVALU

Tuvalu's flag is based on the Blue Ensign (see page 109), reflecting the country's historical links with the United Kingdom. The yellow stars are arranged as a map of Tuvalu's nine islands, with east at the top.

VANUATU

Adopted in 1980, the Vanuatu flag is a pall, a Y-shaped design that in this case represents the islands' shape on the map. The flag's colors symbolize nature (green), shared blood (red), and people (black).

FIJI

Based on the Blue Ensign, the flag of Fiji is charged with the shield from the national coat of arms. The flag was adopted in 1970 when the country gained independence from the United Kingdom.

TONGA

Tonga's flag features a red cross in its upper left canton, representing Christianity, the religion of the majority of the islands' people. The flag's red symbolizes the blood of Christ, while the white stands for purity.

SAMOA

Flown since 1949, the flag of Samoa features the Southern Cross (see page 110) in a blue rectangle in the upper left canton, on a red field. White stands for purity, blue for freedom, and red for bravery.

DID YOU KNOW? From 1862 to 1866, the Tonga flag was a red cross on a white field, which is so similar to the flag of the Red Cross charity (see page 26) that it was changed.

The Equator

The flags of two Pacific Island nations, the Marshall Islands and Nauru, depict the equator. Two other equatorial countries also represent the equator on their flags: Brazil, as a band containing a motto; and Gabon, as a yellow stripe. In the flag of the Marshall Islands, the equator is represented by an orange and white diagonal band. A large white star above the band represents the islands' position just north of the equator. In the flag of Nauru, which lies south of the equator, a white star is positioned under a yellow stripe.

The Marshall Islands are composed of more than 1,150 islands and islets, many of them formed from coral reefs.

In mating season, the male great frigatebird inflates his red throat sac.

FLAG FOCUS: Pacific Community

Type: International organization

In use: 1999–present

Flown by: 26 countries and territories in Oceania, which work together on education, farming, fishing, and medical projects

Design: The 26 stars represent the 26 members, which are joined by a turquoise arch, representing the organization itself. The central design signifies a sail and ocean waves, suggesting progress, as well as a palm tree, representing the region's wealth. The colors reflect the night sky and ocean.

The male waggles
his head, shakes
his wings,
and calls.

Dancing Frigatebirds

The flag of Kiribati depicts a great frigatebird, a large seabird that flies great distances across tropical regions of the world's oceans. The bird nests on the islands of Kiribati, where males can be seen dancing with stretched wings to attract a female. On Kiribati's flag, the bird represents freedom as well as the nation's traditional dances, which feature outstretched arms and sudden bird-like movements of the head.

A dancer tests her strength by holding her arms outstretched, like wings, for long periods.

DID YOU KNOW? The flag of Fiji depicts four of the islands' most important crops in its shield: a cocoa pod, sugar cane, coconut palm, and bananas.

115

Atlantic and Arctic Oceans: Territories

Scattered across these oceans are several overseas territories, which form part of a distant country. Some territories govern themselves and make their own laws, while others are governed directly by their parent country. Seventeen of these territories have their own official flag (shown here), while others, such as France's St. Barthélemy, fly the flag of their parent country.

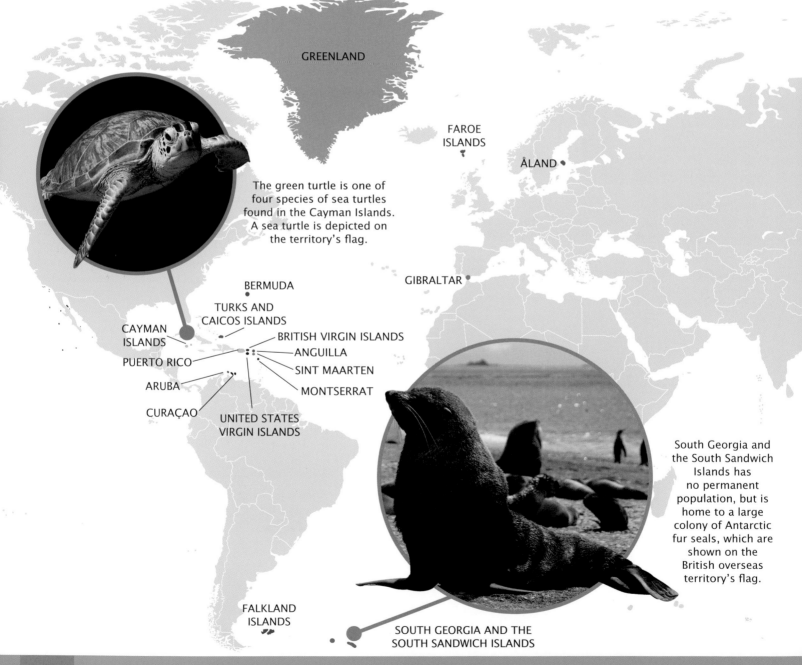

GREENLAND

FAROE ISLANDS

ÅLAND

The green turtle is one of four species of sea turtles found in the Cayman Islands. A sea turtle is depicted on the territory's flag.

GIBRALTAR

BERMUDA

TURKS AND CAICOS ISLANDS

BRITISH VIRGIN ISLANDS

CAYMAN ISLANDS

ANGUILLA

PUERTO RICO

SINT MAARTEN

ARUBA

MONTSERRAT

CURAÇAO

UNITED STATES VIRGIN ISLANDS

South Georgia and the South Sandwich Islands has no permanent population, but is home to a large colony of Antarctic fur seals, which are shown on the British overseas territory's flag.

FALKLAND ISLANDS

SOUTH GEORGIA AND THE SOUTH SANDWICH ISLANDS

DID YOU KNOW? The Puerto Rico flag was modeled on the red, white, and blue flag of Cuba, which also features horizontal stripes and a starred triangle at the hoist.

GREENLAND

Designed in 1989, the flag of Greenland (see page 118) uses the colors of the flag of Denmark, of which Greenland is a self-governing part.

FAROE ISLANDS

A constituent country of Denmark, the Faroe Islands flies a Nordic Cross flag, like most of the Nordic countries and territories (see page 74).

ÅLAND

Åland is a self-governing region of Finland where most people speak Swedish. It flies a Nordic cross in the colors of both Sweden and Finland.

GIBRALTAR

Gibraltar is the only British overseas territory that does not bear the Union Jack on its flag. The castle represents Gibraltar's fortifications.

BERMUDA

Unlike most British overseas territories, Bermuda has a flag with a red field. It features Bermuda's coat of arms, which depicts a shipwreck.

CAYMAN ISLANDS

Based on the Blue Ensign (see page 109), this flag features the territory's coat of arms, which bears a star for each of the main islands.

TURKS AND CAICOS ISLANDS

The coat of arms of Turks and Caicos features a conch shell, lobster, and cactus, representing the islands' natural world.

BRITISH VIRGIN ISLANDS

This territory's coat of arms depicts St. Ursula, the young woman ("virgin") after whom the islands are named.

ANGUILLA

Anguilla's coat of arms features three leaping dolphins, representing wisdom, strength, and friendship.

PUERTO RICO

A United States territory, Puerto Rico has flown this flag since 1952. The star represents the island, while the blue symbolizes the sea.

UNITED STATES VIRGIN ISLANDS

Adopted in 1921, this flag features a simplified United States coat of arms, between a V and I (for Virgin Islands).

SINT MAARTEN

This flag features the constituent country's coat of arms (see page 119), on white (for purity), red (courage), and blue (peace).

MONTSERRAT

Montserrat's coat of arms depicts a woman holding a harp, a symbol of Ireland (see page 71), reflecting many of the islanders' Irish roots.

ARUBA

A constituent country of the Netherlands, Aruba uses blue to signify ocean, yellow for freedom, and a red star for the island's people.

CURAÇAO

Part of the Netherlands, Curaçao uses two stars to depict its two islands, a yellow stripe for the sun, and blue for the ocean.

FALKLAND ISLANDS

Adopted in 1999, this flag displays the islands' coat of arms, which depicts a ram to represent the important industry of sheep farming.

SOUTH GEORGIA AND THE SOUTH SANDWICH ISLANDS

This territory's coat of arms includes depictions of a lion and three animals found on the islands: a reindeer, fur seal, and macaroni penguin.

Glaciers and Icebergs

With an area of 836,000 sq miles (2.2 million sq km), Greenland is the world's largest territory. The island's average daily temperature is above freezing only in June, July, and August. Most of Greenland's 56,000 inhabitants live along the warmer southwest coast. The flag of Greenland depicts the country's ice sheet and icebergs. The white stripe represents the ice sheet, which covers four-fifth of the island's land. The red semicircle and stripe represent the sun and the ocean. The white semicircle represents icebergs, which break off from glaciers where they meet the ocean or lakes. Glaciers are rivers of ice that flow slowly downhill.

Having broken from Jakobshavn Glacier, icebergs float past Ilulissat Church in western Greenland.

In the Faroe Islands, children wave Faroe Islands and Danish flags as they wait for a visit by the Danish royal family.

DID YOU KNOW? By coincidence, the flag of Greenland is almost identical to the flag of Danish rowing club HEI Rosport.

An Important Building

The flag of Sint Maarten is one of six national flags (Afghanistan, Bolivia, Cambodia, Portugal, San Marino, and Spain) and two territory flags (including Gibraltar) that display a building. The building on Sint Maarten's flag is its Constitutional Courthouse, where judges decide on whether laws put forward by the parliament of Sint Maarten are fair and legal. Sint Maarten is a constituent country of the Netherlands. A constituent country is part of a larger country but has independence on issues that relate only to itself.

Sint Maarten's courthouse
was built in 1793.

The flag of the
Faroe Islands
was adopted
in 1940.

Indian and Pacific Oceans: Territories

Thirteen of the islands and island groups of the Indian and Pacific Oceans are overseas territories that fly their own flags. Many of these flags feature their islands' plants, which provide food or materials for construction and art. Three flags depict palm trees, while Norfolk Island shows its native evergreen tree. The Pitcairn Islands flag shows Pacific rosewood, while the Northern Mariana Islands depicts a *mwarmwar*, a traditional wreath of local flowers.

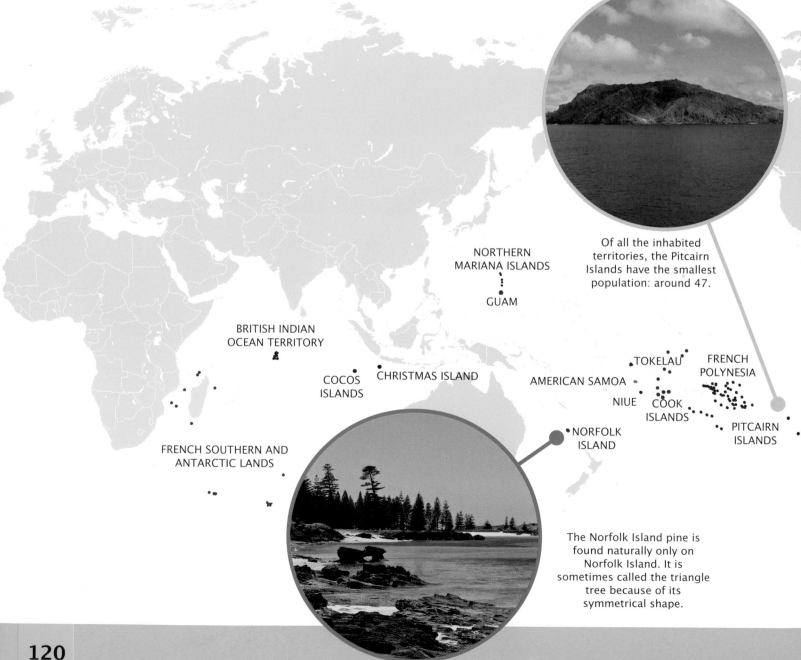

Of all the inhabited territories, the Pitcairn Islands have the smallest population: around 47.

NORTHERN MARIANA ISLANDS

GUAM

BRITISH INDIAN OCEAN TERRITORY

COCOS ISLANDS

CHRISTMAS ISLAND

AMERICAN SAMOA

TOKELAU

FRENCH POLYNESIA

NIUE

COOK ISLANDS

PITCAIRN ISLANDS

NORFOLK ISLAND

FRENCH SOUTHERN AND ANTARCTIC LANDS

The Norfolk Island pine is found naturally only on Norfolk Island. It is sometimes called the triangle tree because of its symmetrical shape.

BRITISH INDIAN OCEAN TERRITORY

Adopted in 1990, this flag represents the Indian Ocean with blue waving lines. In the fly is a palm tree and St Edward's Crown, part of the crown jewels of the United Kingdom.

COCOS (KEELING) ISLANDS

An Australian external territory, Cocos Islands flies a green flag with a Southern Cross (see page 110) in the fly. The crescent moon represents Islam, while the palm tree signifies the islands' plant life.

CHRISTMAS ISLAND

Christmas Island, an Australian external territory, displays the Southern Cross (see page 110), a map of the island in a yellow circle, and the outline of a golden bosun bird, which nests only on the island.

FRENCH SOUTHERN AND ANTARCTIC LANDS

In the fly, the letters TAAF (from the French name for the territory: Terres Australes et Antarctiques Françaises) form a monogram (a symbol made by combining letters).

NORTHERN MARIANA ISLANDS

This territory of the United States flies a flag featuring a *mwarmwar*, a stone sculpture known as a *latte*, erected on the islands since around 900 CE; and a star representing the United States.

GUAM

A territory of the United States, Guam has a blue flag with a red border, representing the blood spilt in World War II. The seal at the center shows a traditional boat (see page 122) sailing in the island's Hagåtña Bay.

TOKELAU

A territory of New Zealand, Tokelau flies a flag depicting the Southern Cross (see page 110) and a traditional sailing boat (see page 122). The flag was adopted in 2009.

AMERICAN SAMOA

The only inhabited United States territory south of the equator, American Samoa has a flag featuring the bald eagle, the US national bird. Red, white, and blue are the colors of the US flag as well as traditional Samoan colors.

NIUE

Niue is a self-governing country in association with New Zealand. The Union Jack reflects Niue's relationships with the United Kingdom and New Zealand. The yellow field expresses sunshine and kindness.

COOK ISLANDS

The design of the Cook Islands' flag reflects the flag of New Zealand, with which this self-governing country is in association. The 15 stars stand for the country's 15 islands.

FRENCH POLYNESIA

Adopted in 1984, the flag of French Polynesia depicts a traditional boat (see page 122) on a pattern representing ocean waves and the rays of a rising sun.

PITCAIRN ISLANDS

The flag of this British overseas territory displays the islands' coat of arms (see page 123). Above the shield is a local wheelbarrow, signifying hard work.

NORFOLK ISLAND

An external territory of Australia, Norfolk Island flies a flag charged with a native tree (see opposite). The two green stripes represent the island's natural world.

DID YOU KNOW? Only the islands of Christmas Island and Cyprus feature a map of the island itself on their flags.

Brave Boats

The flags of three Pacific Island groups, French Polynesia, Guam, and Tokelau, depict traditional boats. The flags of both French Polynesia and Guam display a wooden sailing boat with two hulls (or bodies). The flag of Tokelau shows a simplified canoe sailing toward the Southern Cross. Traditional Pacific Island boats are hollowed from the trunks of trees. While some have two hulls for balance, others have outriggers, or floats, to keep them stable. It was in such sailing boats that the first settlers of the Pacific Islands traveled from Asia, reaching Guam in around 1500 BCE and French Polynesia in around 700 CE.

The American eagle holds a war club and fly swat, both symbols of Samoan leaders.

This single-hulled boat has an outrigger.

FLAG FOCUS: Marquesas Islands

Type: Region

In use: 1980–present

Flown by: The Marquesas Islands, an island group in French Polynesia

Design: The colors of the flag are traditional: Yellow represents festivals, while white and red are sacred colors of chiefs. In the white triangle is a black Tiki, a representation of the first human in Marquesas mythology, who invented the arts of sculpture and tattooing.

DID YOU KNOW? The five star-like shapes on French Polynesia's canoe represent passengers, each standing for one of the French overseas country's five island groups.

Mutiny on the Bounty

The Pitcairn Islands' flag displays a shield decorated with an anchor and Bible from the ship HMS *Bounty*. In 1789, 22 of the sailors on board this British ship mutinied (or rebelled) against their captain, William Bligh. The mutineers, led by Fletcher Christian, forced the captain and those loyal to him off the *Bounty* and into a small supply boat. Nine mutineers, along with several local men and women, landed on uninhabited Pitcairn, where they settled. Some of their descendants live on the island today.

Captain Bligh is held at gunpoint by the mutineers. The captain and his men later sailed to safety in Indonesia.

Antarctica

Earth's southernmost continent, Antarctica is not the possession of any country and does not have its own official flag. The continent is jointly governed by the 54 countries that have agreed the Antarctic Treaty, which sets down rules to protect Antarctica's environment. Around 40 countries have scientific research stations in Antarctica, which often fly their own national flags.

A Flag for Antarctica

Several flags have been suggested for Antarctica. Although none has been officially adopted, two have become popular. While working in Antarctica, Evan Townsend designed the True South flag. Horizontal stripes of navy and white represent the long summer days and winter nights in Antarctica, when the sun either never dips below the horizon or never rises. In the center of the flag, a white peak represents the continent's mountains, while with its shadow it forms the shape of a compass arrow pointing south. The second flag, designed by vexillologist Graham Bartram, shows the shape of the continent in purewhite, symbolizing Antarctica's freedom from ownership.

The True South flag is flown at several Antarctic research stations.

The Graham Bartram flag flutters on the prow of a visiting cruise ship.

The 12 countries that first signed the Antarctic Treaty display their national flags.

DID YOU KNOW? In 2007, a submarine planted the Russian flag on the seabed at the North Pole, which lies in the middle of the Arctic Ocean.

Reaching the South Pole

The Norwegian flag was the first national flag planted at the South Pole. Led by Roald Amundsen, a Norwegian team of five men and 16 sled dogs reached the Pole on December 14, 1911. The second national flag was the United Kingdom's, planted a month later by Robert Falcon Scott and four others, all of whom died on the return journey.

Amundsen and his men admire their flags at the South Pole: The Norwegian flag flies above the flag of their ship, the *Fram*.

The ceremonial South Pole, a few yards from the true South Pole, is used for photos.

FLAG FOCUS:
Antarctic Treaty

Type: International organization

In use: 2002–present

Flown by: The 54 countries that have agreed the Antarctic Treaty

Design: The white outline of the Antarctic continent appears on a navy blue field. It is marked with the main lines of latitude (circling the South Pole) and longitude (running away from the Pole), used to pinpoint locations on Earth's surface.

Glossary

ARAB LIBERATION COLORS
Red, white, and black; these colors were inspired by the Arab Liberation Flag flown during the Egyptian Revolution of 1952.

ARAB PEOPLES
People who speak Arabic and historically live in western Asia and northern and eastern Africa.

BUDDHISM
A religion based on the teachings of Siddhartha Guatama, the Buddha, who lived in India between the 6th and 4th centuries BCE.

CANTON
A rectangular area of a flag, occupying up to a quarter of the flag, usually at the top hoist (left) corner.

CHARGE
An emblem, object, or design placed on the field of a flag.

CHEVRON
A V-shaped design on a flag.

CHRISTIANITY
A religion based on the teachings of Jesus Christ, including the Catholic, Protestant, and Eastern Orthodox Churches.

COAT OF ARMS
A design in the form of a shield, used to symbolize a family, organization, town, or country.

COMMUNISM
A system of government in which all property, such as businesses, is owned by the community.

CONSTELLATION
A group of stars that, when viewed from Earth, seem to form the shape of an object or person.

CONSTITUENT COUNTRY
A country that forms part of a larger country.

COUNTRY
An area of land with its own government that has control over the country's own affairs.

CREST
A tuft of feathers or other design at the top of a helmet.

DEMOCRACY
A system of government in which the people get a say in law-making, usually by voting for their representatives in a parliament.

DEPENDENCY
An area of land that is governed by another, usually distant, country. A dependency often has control over many of its own affairs.

DISCIPLE
A follower of Jesus Christ during his lifetime.

DYNASTY
A series of rulers who are all from the same family.

EMBLAZON
To display a coat of arms or other design on a flag's field.

EMBLEM
An object or design that represents a person, group, or country.

EMPIRE
A group of countries that are governed by one ruler or country.

ENSIGN
A national flag flown on a ship.

FESS
A horizontal band across the center of a flag.

FIELD
The background of a flag.

FIMBRIATION
Small stripes in a contrasting color, along the edges of symbols or stripes.

FLY
The edge, or half, of a flag farthest from the flagpole.

GOVERNMENT
A group of people who are responsible for a country or state.

HERALDRY
The design and study of coats of arms, crests, and mottoes.

HINDUISM
A religion that grew in India after 500 BCE, with a belief in one God who takes many forms that may be worshiped as different gods.

HOIST
The edge, or half, of a flag nearest to the flagpole.

ISLAM
A religion based on the teachings of the Prophet Muhammad, who was born in Mecca, in modern Saudi Arabia, in around 570 CE.

JACK
A flag flown from a short staff at the bow (front) of a ship. An ensign is flown at the stern (rear).

JAINISM
A religion that grew up in India in around the 6th century BCE, based on the importance of non-violence and self-discipline.

JUDAISM
A religion that developed in the region of modern Israel from around 2000 BCE.

LOGO
A symbol or simple design that represents a person or organization.

MAMMAL
An animal with hair or fur; female mammals feed their babies on milk.

MIDDLE AGES
A period in European history lasting from around 500 to 1500 CE.

MOTTO
A short sentence or phrase that expresses the beliefs or hopes of a person, group, or country.

MYTHOLOGICAL
Described in myths, which are traditional stories about gods and heroes or explaining the natural world.

NATIONAL FLAG
A flag that represents a country, flown by its government and usually also by its citizens.

NATIVE
Belonging in a particular place.

NAVIGATION
Finding and following an exact route from one place to another.

NAVY
The branch of a country's armed forces that travels by water.

NORDIC CROSS
A cross that has vertical and horizontal arms, with the center of the cross closer to the flag's hoist than the fly.

OVERSEAS TERRITORY
An area of land that is governed by another country, from which it is separated by ocean.

PAN-AFRICAN COLORS
Green, yellow, and red; these colors were inspired by the flag of Ethiopia and represent the goal of strength and unity between African peoples.

PAN-ARAB COLORS
Red, white, black, and green; each color represents a different Arab dynasty, together symbolizing the unity of Arab peoples.

PARLIAMENT
A group of people who meet to decide on a country's laws, oversee its government, and represent the population.

PATRON SAINT
In Christianity, a holy person who is linked to, or believed to offer protection to, a particular group or place.

PENNON
Also called a pennant, a flag that is larger at the hoist than at the fly, often with a triangular shape or with separate "tongues" called swallowtails.

POPULATION
All the people who live in a particular place.

PROPORTION
The ratio of a flag's (vertical) height to its (horizontal) width. A ratio of 1:2 means that the height (1) is half the width (2).

REPUBLIC
A country without a king or queen, where power is shared by the people and their elected representatives.

REVOLUTION
The overthrow of a government in favor of a new system.

SALTIRE
A diagonal cross, like a letter X, on a flag.

STANDARD
A flag that, historically, was flown by an army, king, or queen as a means of identification.

TRIBAND
A flag with three parallel bands of color, with the bands either horizontal or vertical.

TRICOLOR
A triband flag with bands of three different colors. Tricolors were often adopted as symbols of freedom or revolution.

UNITY
Being together or in agreement.

VARIANT FLAG
A different, official national flag. Common variants are civil flags, which may be flown by anyone; state flags, flown by government agencies; and war or military flags, flown by armies and air forces.

VEXILLOLOGIST
A person who studies the designs, history, and use of flags.

Index